SUMMER BRAIN QUEST®

Dear Parent,

At Brain Quest, we believe learning should be an adventure—a *quest* for knowledge. Our mission has always been to guide children on that quest, to keep them excited, motivated, and curious, and to give them the confidence they need to do well in school. Now, we're extending the quest to summer! Meet SUMMER BRAIN QUEST: It's a workbook. It's a game. It's an outdoor adventure. And it's going to stop summer slide!

Research shows that if kids take a break from learning all summer, they can lose up to three months' worth of knowledge from the previous grade. So we set out to create a one-of-a-kind workbook experience that delivers personalized learning for every kind of kid. Personalized learning is an educational method where exercises are tailored to each child's strengths, needs, and interests. Our goal was to empower kids to have a voice in what and how they learned during the summer, while ensuring they get enough practice with the fundamentals. The result: SUMMER BRAIN QUEST—a complete interactive program that is easy to use and designed to engage each unique kid all summer long.

So how does it work? Each SUMMER BRAIN QUEST WORKBOOK includes a pullout tri-fold map that functions as a game board, progress chart, and personalized learning system. Our map shows different routes that correspond to over 100 pages of curriculum-based exercises and 8 outdoor learning experiences. The variety of routes enables kids to choose different topics and activities while guaranteeing practice in weaker skills. We've also included over 150 stickers to mark progress, incentivize challenging exercises, and celebrate accomplishments. As kids complete activities and earn stickers, they can put them wherever they like on the map, so each child's map is truly unique—just like your kid. To top it all off, we included a Summer Brainiac Award to mark your child's successful completion of his or her quest. SUMMER BRAIN QUEST guides kids so they feel supported, and it offers positive feedback and builds confidence by showing kids how far they've come and just how much they've learned.

Each SUMMER BRAIN QUEST WORKBOOK has been created in consultation with an award-winning teacher specializing in that grade. We cover the core competencies of reading, writing, and math, as well as the essentials of social studies and science. We ensure that our exercises are aligned to Common Core State Standards, Next Generation Science Standards, and state social studies standards.

Loved by kids and adored by teachers, Brain Quest is America's #1 educational bestseller and has been an important bridge to the classroom for millions of children. SUMMER BRAIN QUEST is an effective new tool for parents, homeschoolers, tutors, and teachers alike to stop summer slide. By providing fun, personalized, and meaningful educational materials, our mission is to help ALL kids keep their skills ALL summer long. Most of all, we want kids to know:

It's your summer. It's your workbook. It's your learning adventure.

—The editors of Brain Quest

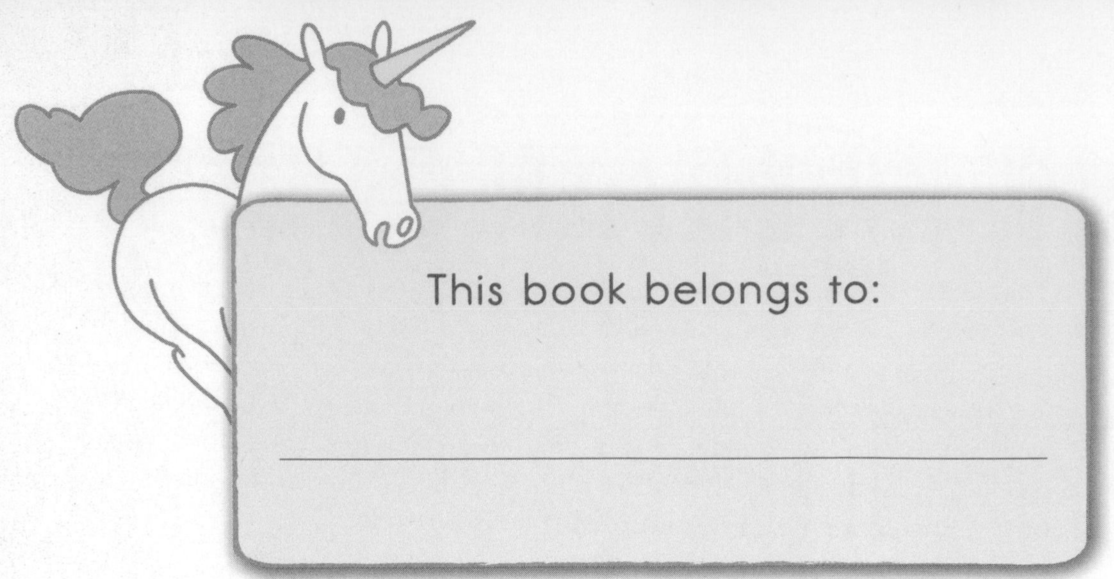

Library of Congress Cataloging-in-Publication Data is available.

ISBN 978-0-7611-8919-0

Summer Series Concept by Nathalie Le Du, Daniel Nayeri, Tim Hall
Writers Persephone Walker, Claire Piddock
Consulting Editor Jackie Bonilla
Art Director Colleen AF Venable
Cover, Map, Additional Character, and Interior Illustrator Edison Yan
Series Designer Tim Hall
Designers Abby Dening, Gordon Whiteside
Editor Nathalie Le Du
Production Editor Jessica Rozler
Production Manager Julie Primavera

Workman Publishing Co., Inc.
225 Varick Street
New York, NY 10014-4381
workman.com

Printed in the United States of America
First printing March 2017

10 9 8 7 6 5 4

BETWEEN GRADES 3&4

For adventurers ages 8–9

Written by Persephone Walker and Claire Piddock
Consulting Editor: Jackie Bonilla

WORKMAN PUBLISHING
NEW YORK

Contents

SUMMER BRAIN QUEST®
BETWEEN GRADES 3 & 4

Your Quest

Your quest is to sticker as many paths on the map as possible and reach the final destination by the end of summer to become an official Summer Brainiac.

Basic Components

Summer progress map

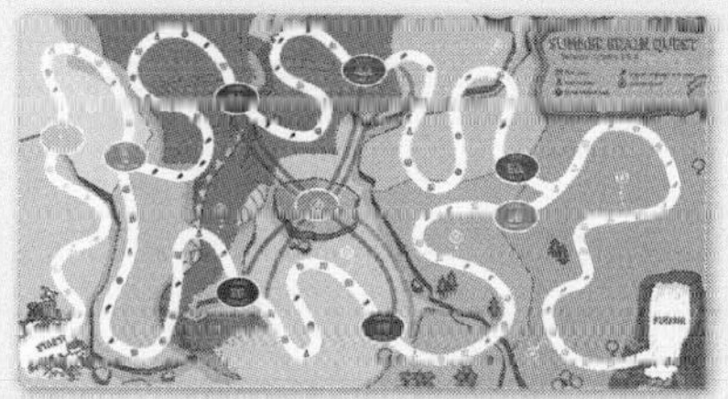

100+ pages of exercises

100+ quest stickers

8 Outside Quests

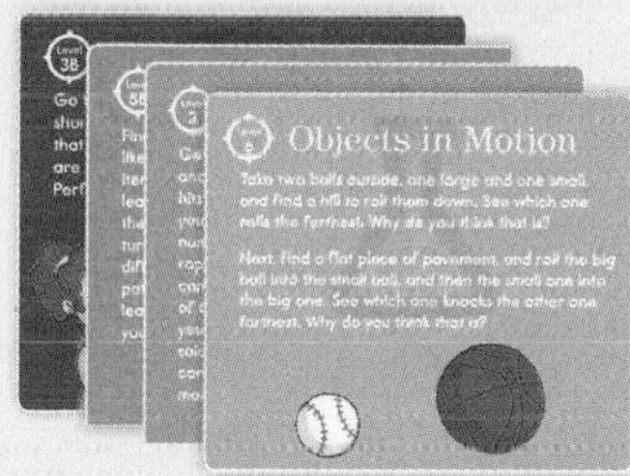
Objects in Motion

8 Outside Quest stickers

Over 30 achievement stickers

Summer Brainiac Award

Summer Brainiac Award
Presented to:
for successfully completing the learning journey in
Summer Brain Quest: Between Grades 3&4

100% sticker

Setup

Detach the map and place it on a flat surface.

Begin at **START** on your map.

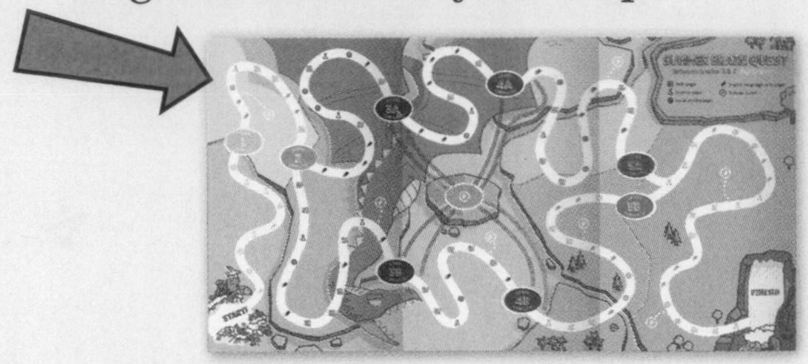

How to Play

To advance along a path, you must complete a quest exercise with the matching color and symbol. For example:

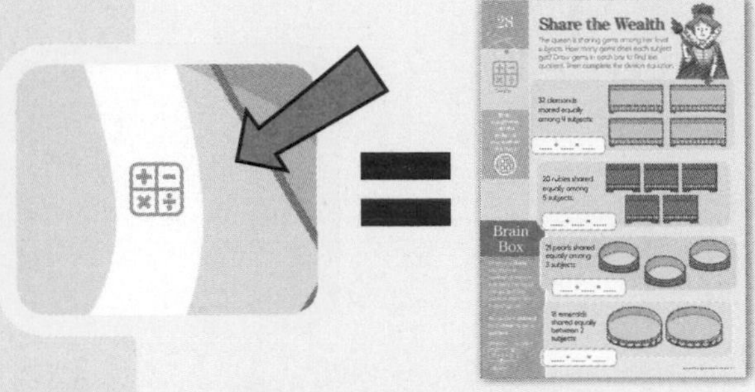

Math exercise from the orange level (Level 2)

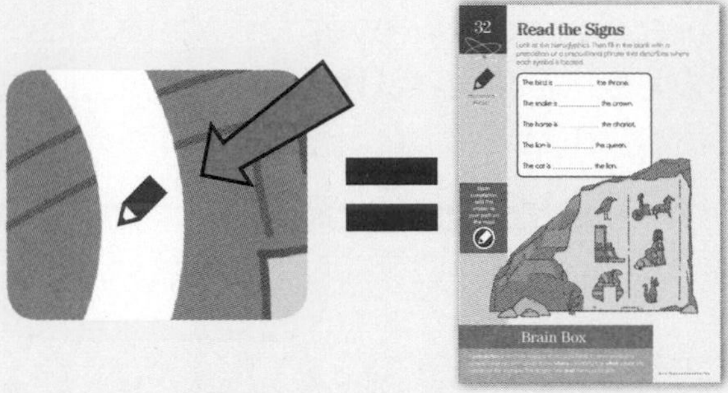

English language arts exercise from the red level (Level 3A)

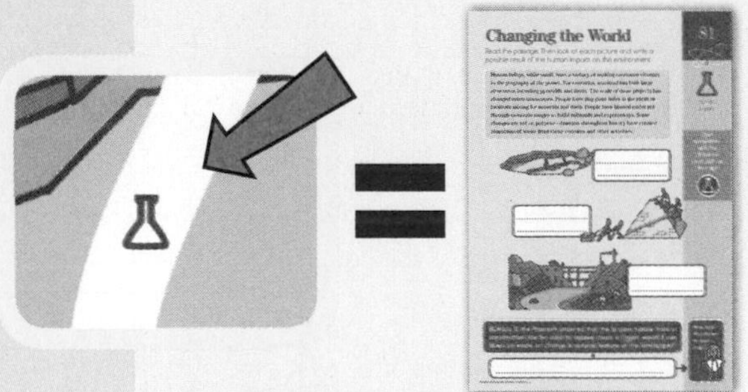

Science exercise from the blue level (Level 5A)

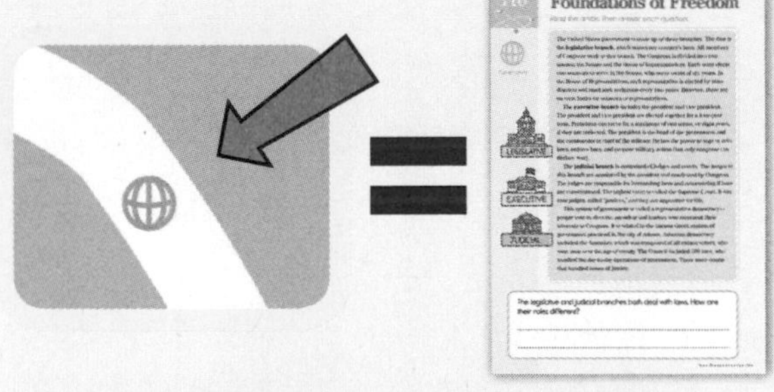

Social studies exercise from the green level (Level 6)

If you complete the challenge, you earn a matching quest sticker.

Place the quest sticker on the path to continue on your journey.

At the end of each leg of your journey, you earn an achievement sticker.

Apply it to the map and move on to the next level!

Forks in Your Path

When you reach a fork in your path, you can choose which direction to take. However, each level must be completed in its entirety. For example, you cannot lay two quest stickers down on Level 3A and then switch to Level 3B.

If you complete one level, you can return to the fork in the path and complete the other level.

Outside Quests

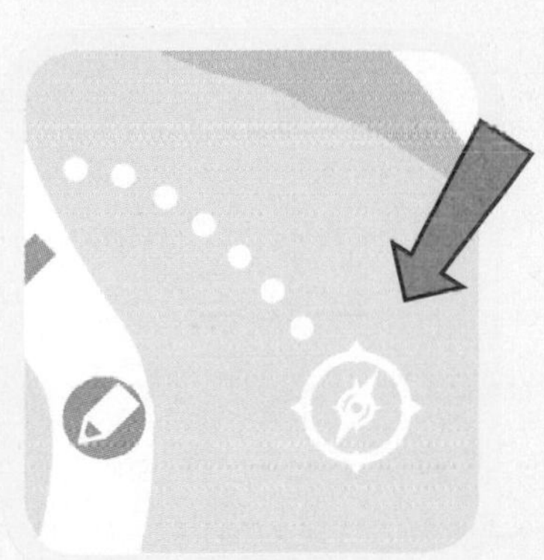

Throughout the map, you will encounter paths that lead to Outside Quests.

To advance along those paths, you must complete one of the Outside Quests.

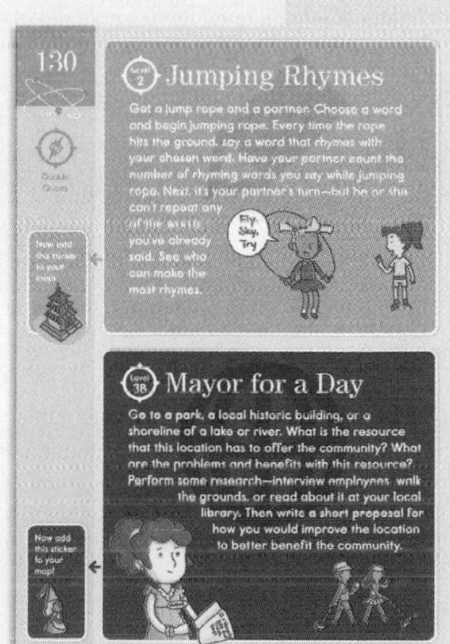

130

Level 2 Jumping Rhymes

Get a jump rope and a partner. Choose a word and begin jumping rope. Every time the rope hits the ground, say a word that rhymes with your chosen word. Have your partner count the number of rhyming words you say while jumping rope. Next, it's your partner's turn—but he or she can't repeat any of the words you've already said. See who can make the most rhymes.

Level 3B Mayor for a Day

Go to a park, a local historic building, or a shoreline of a lake or river. What is the resource that this location has to offer the community? What are the problems and benefits with this resource? Perform some research—interview employees, walk the grounds, or read about it at your local library. Then write a short proposal for how you would improve the location to better benefit the community.

Now add this sticker to your map!

If you complete an Outside Quest, you earn an Outside Quest sticker and advance toward 100% completion!

Bonuses

If you complete a bonus question, you earn an achievement sticker.

BONUS: If Troy existed today, in what country would it be located?

Now add this sticker to your map!

Subject Completion

If you complete all of the quest exercises in a subject (math, English language arts, science, or social studies), you earn an achievement sticker.

CONGRATULATIONS!
You completed all of your science quests! You earned:

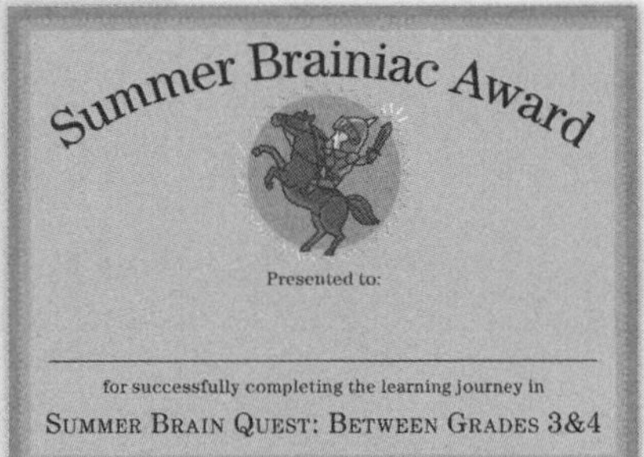

Summer Brainiac Award
Presented to:
for successfully completing the learning journey in
Summer Brain Quest: Between Grades 3&4

Summer Brain Quest Completion Sticker and Award

If you complete your quest, you earn a Summer Brain Quest completion sticker and award!

100% Sticker

Sticker *every* possible route and finish *all* the Outside Quests to earn the 100% sticker!

Level 1

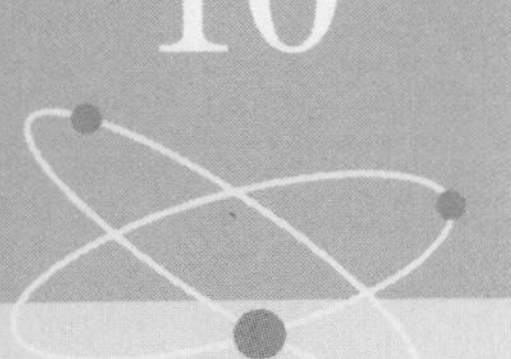

Fragments and Run-on Sentences

Upon completion, add this sticker to your path on the map!

Anchors Aweigh!

Circle each complete sentence. Rewrite each fragment or run-on sentence as a complete sentence or sentences.

One of the first ways people traveled the world was by sea.

Canoed and sailed to discover new lands or escape trouble at home.

Sailerls canoed to discover lands
or escape trouble at home

Ancient people crossed vast seas and oceans in all sorts of dugout vessels, they were driven by commerce, conflict, and climate, like seasonal changes in wild plants and game.

From one side of the ocean to the other, exchanged technology, new ways of thinking, agriculture, and arts.

From one side of the ocean
to the other people exchanged
technology find new ways of think ing.

Today, people still cross oceans for many of the same reasons: climate change, political upheaval, and to find a better life.

Brain Box

A **run-on sentence** joins two independent clauses without the correct punctuation or a conjunction such as **and**, **but**, or **because**. A **sentence fragment** is missing a subject or a verb.

The Trading Game

Local Economies

Look at the two communities below. Circle each community's natural resources. Then answer the questions.

Oceanside **Inland**

What are two resources that one community lacks and the other community has?

Oceanside	Inland
fish Seaweeds	Bananas trees

How could they get these resources?

the ocean needs a boot

the inland has a trakter

Upon completion, add this sticker to your path on the map!

Brain Box

Economy describes the resources in a place, what goods people need and buy, and what they have to offer.

Trade is buying, selling, or exchanging goods people have for goods other people want or need.

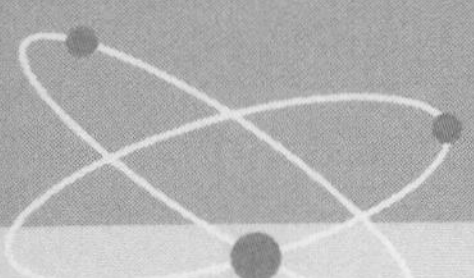

A-Round the Ocean

Rounding Numbers

Round to the nearest hundred.

659

Upon completion, add this sticker to your path on the map!

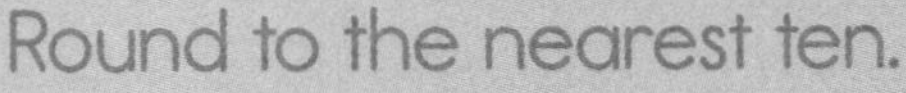

Round to the nearest ten.

444

A fisherman rounded his catch to the nearest ten and wrote 250. What numbers could he have rounded?

2 49

Brain Box

To **round to the nearest hundred**, find the number in the tens place. If it is 5 or greater, round up. If it is 4 or less, round down.

To **round to the nearest ten**, find the number in the ones place. If it is 5 or greater, round up. If it is 4 or less, round down.

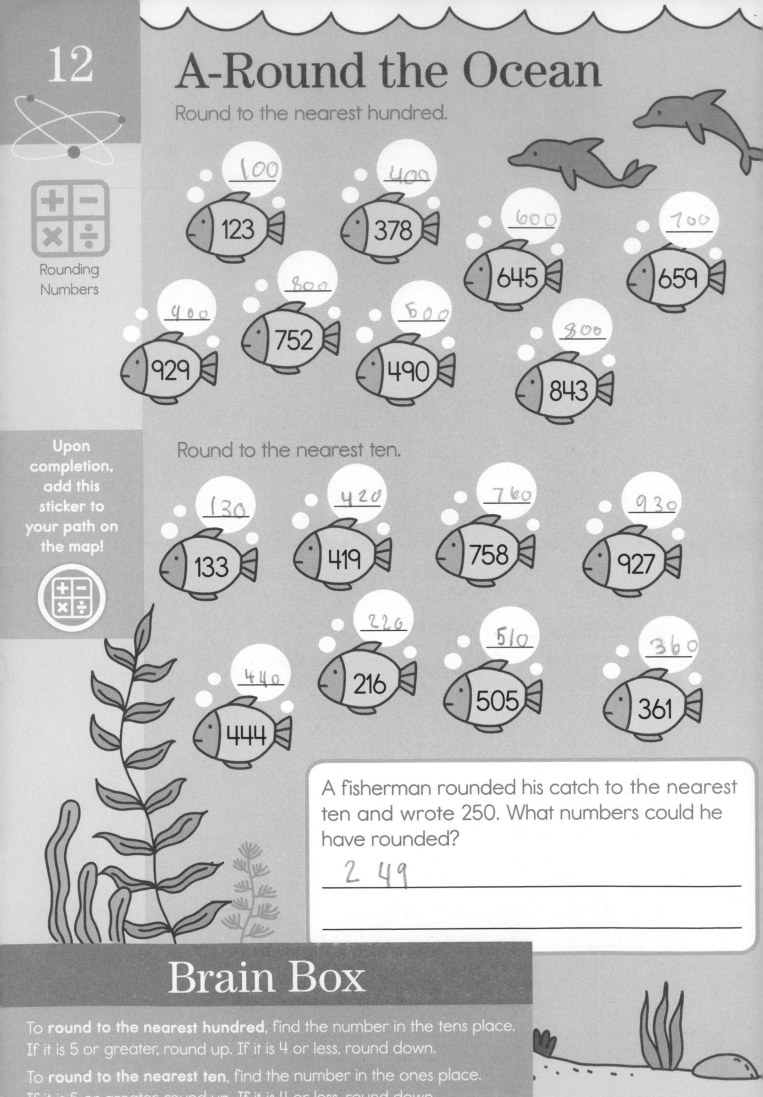

Force of Nature

Read the passage.

Magnetic force occurs when two magnets interact or when one magnet interacts with an electrically charged particle. Magnets can attract or pick up many metal objects, like when a magnet is near something made of iron. The iron will also be attracted to the magnet, and they will move toward each other.

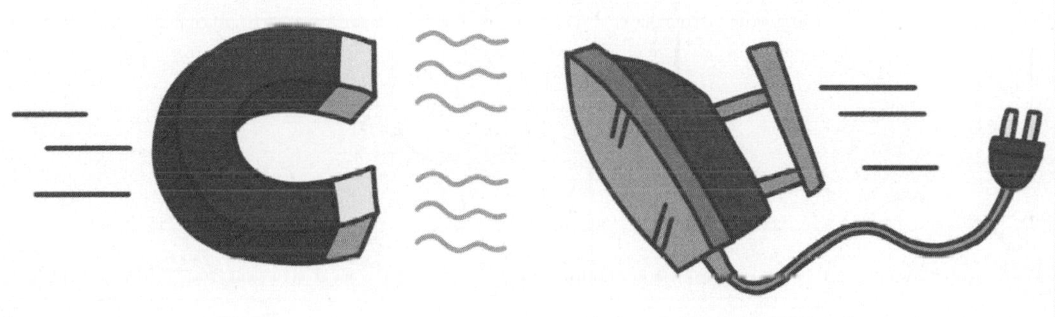

Magnetic Force

Upon completion, add this sticker to your path on the map!

Circle each object that is attracted to or can be picked up by a magnet. Cross out each object that is not magnetic.

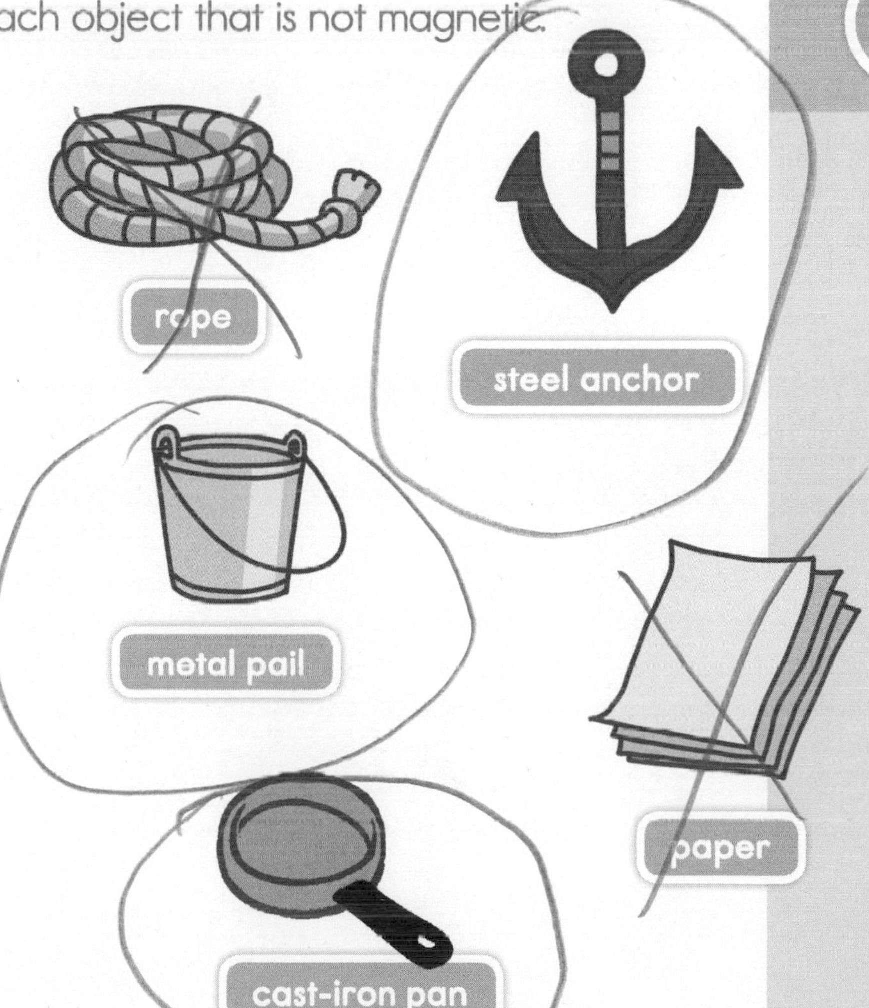

14

Prefixes and Suffixes

Before or After?

Match each prefix or suffix in the box with a root word. Then write the new word and its new definition.

un	or	in	im
dis	under	ful	

water ______________ : ______________________________

visible ______________ : ______________________________

believable ______________ : ______________________________

agree ______________ : ______________________________

power ______________ : ______________________________

sail ______________ : ______________________________

possible ______________ : ______________________________

Upon completion, add this sticker to your path on the map!

Brain Box

A **root word** is a word before any prefixes or suffixes have been added.

A **prefix** is a word segment that changes the meaning of a root word when added to the beginning.

A **suffix** is a word segment that changes the meaning of a root word when added to the end.

BONUS: Fill in the blank with a suffix.

In 1947, Thor Heyerdahl sailed a raft from South America to the Polynesian Islands to show how humans may have migrated across the Pacific Ocean. It was the long______ time anyone had spent on an open boat in modern history.

Now add this sticker to your map!

What Happened Here?

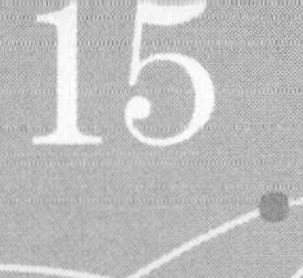

Primary and Secondary Sources

Read each statement about the Sea Queen's stolen trident. Then write whether the statement is from a primary or secondary source.

"I was standing right there when the queen first realized her trident was gone."

____

"I've never seen the underwater police force move so fast."

____

"The *Undersea News* can now report that the queen's advisors claim an arrest will be made soon." ____________________

Upon completion, add this sticker to your path on the map!

"I heard that the queen was so mad she turned blue!"

____

"I didn't tell anyone I saw the princess swim off with the trident, because I didn't want her to get in trouble."

____

Brain Box

A **primary source** provides firsthand information from someone who saw or experienced something directly. These sources can include letters, photographs, or stories from a witness. A **secondary source** provides secondhand information from someone who did not directly see or experience an event. These sources can include textbooks, articles, or biographies from experts and researchers.

16

Circle of Life

Study each creature's life cycle. Then answer each question.

Diverse Life Cycles

Brain Box

A **life cycle** describes the stages that living things go through from birth through the end of life.

Diverse Life Cycles

Which animal doesn't begin life as an egg?

___

Which animal has the fewest life cycle stages?

___

Which animal doesn't only get bigger, but also transforms from one creature into another?

___

Why do you think different animals have different life cycles?

___

Upon completion, add these stickers to your path on the map!

BONUS: Label each member of this Viking family with their stage of development: infant, child, adolescent, and adult.

___

___ ___ ___

Now add this sticker to your map!

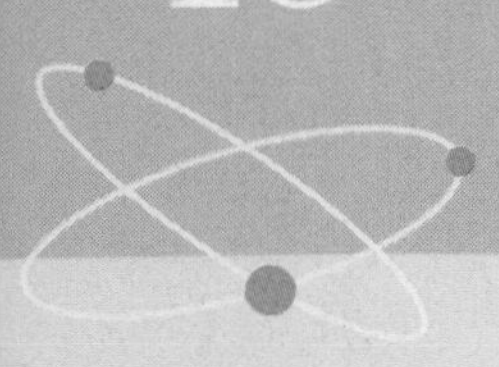

Multiplication: Groups

Exploring Groups

How many groups are there, and how many objects are in each group? Fill in the factors and find the product.

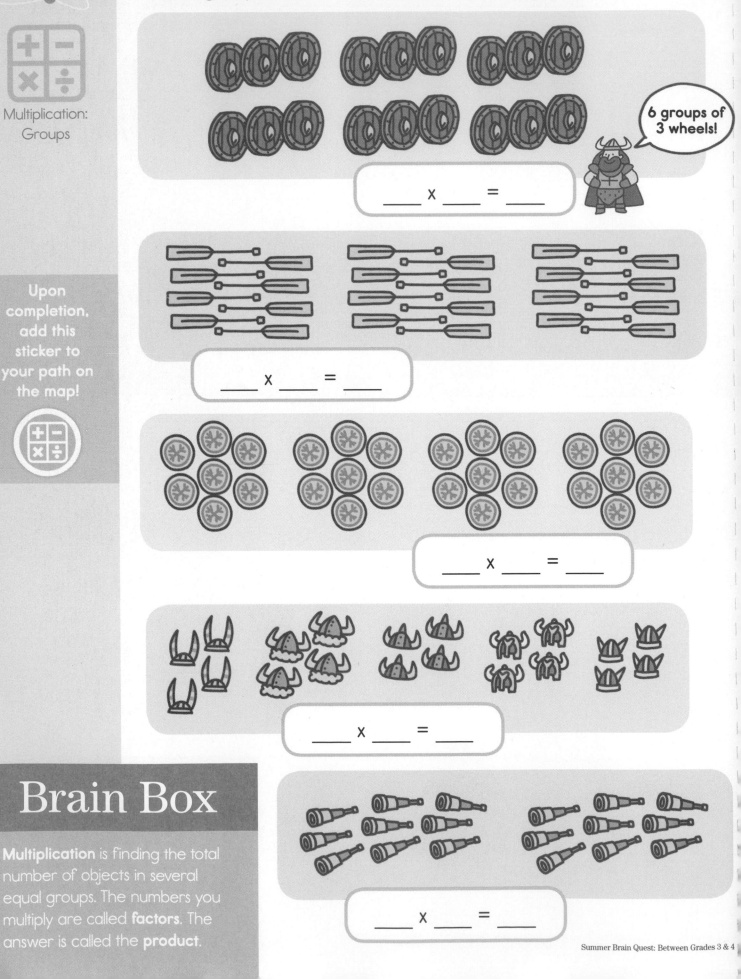

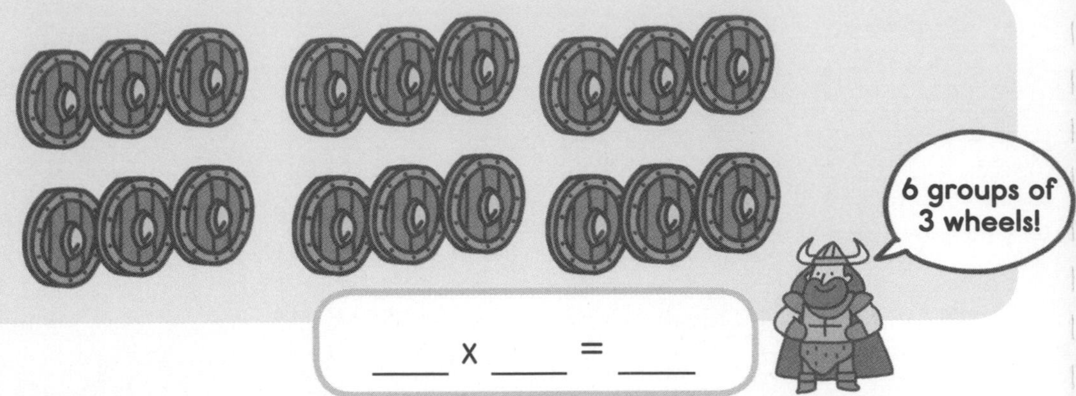

____ x ____ = ____

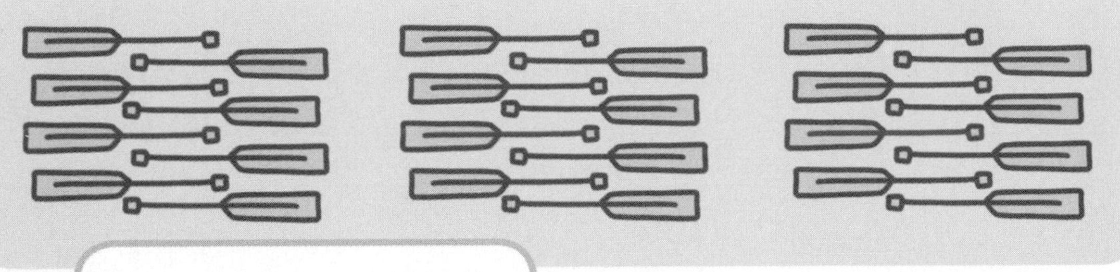

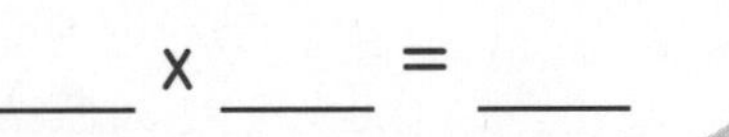

____ x ____ = ____

Upon completion, add this sticker to your path on the map!

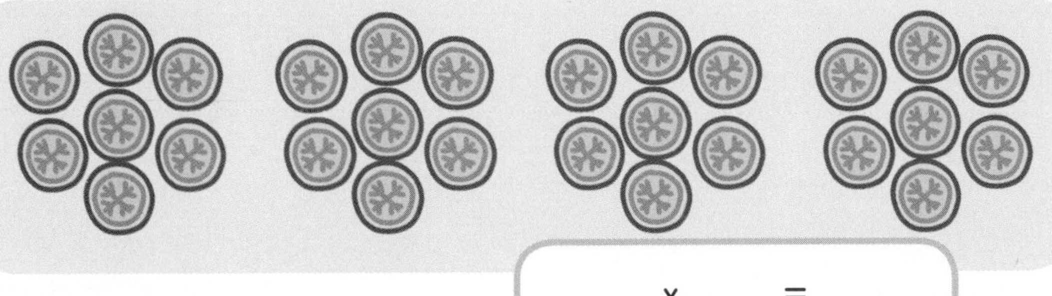

____ x ____ = ____

____ x ____ = ____

Brain Box

Multiplication is finding the total number of objects in several equal groups. The numbers you multiply are called **factors**. The answer is called the **product**.

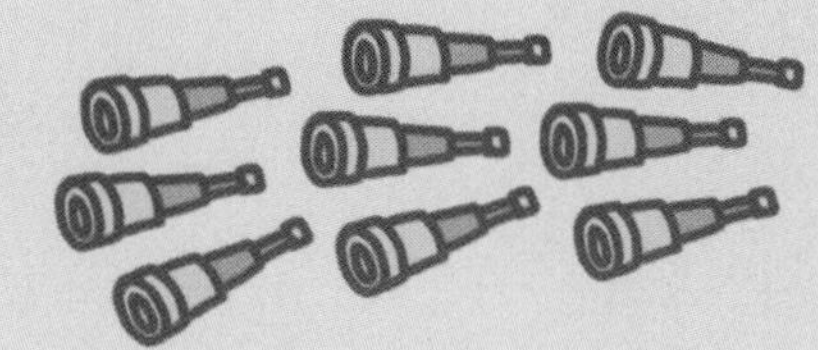

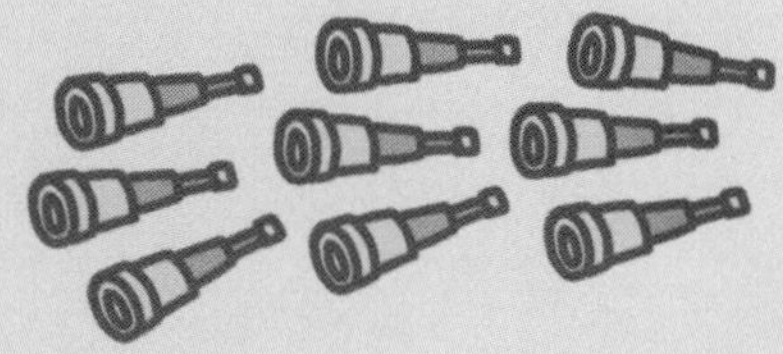

____ x ____ = ____

Level 1 complete!

Add this achievement sticker to your path…

…and move on to

Level 2!

20

Floating into the Past

Circle the present-tense verbs in each sentence. Then rewrite each sentence in the past tense.

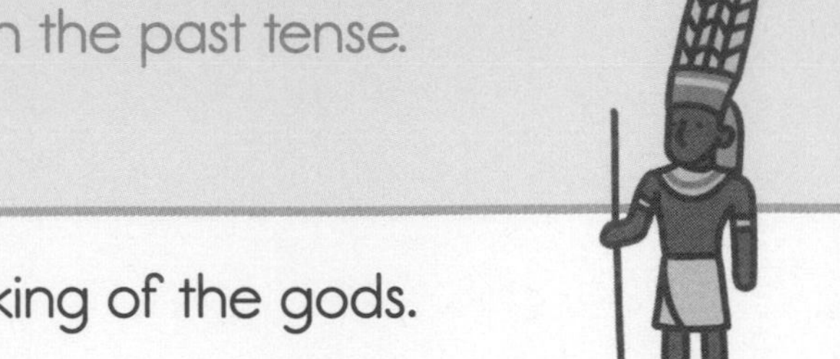

Irregular Verbs

Amon is the ancient Egyptian king of the gods.

____

Mut, or Mother, wears two crowns, one for Upper Egypt and one for Lower Egypt.

____

____

Ancient Egyptians believe that Ra, God of the Sun, is reborn every day.

____

____

The Opet Festival is a boat parade that brings statues of three gods to the temple of Luxor.

____

____

____

Brain Box

Most **verbs** can be changed to the **past tense** by adding **d** or **ed**.

Irregular verbs have a special form in the past tense:

Some change their vowel. Examples: **drink** = **drank**, **fall** = **fell**

Some change their last letter. Examples: **bend** = **bent**, **lose** = **lost**

Some change completely. Examples: **see** = **saw**, **go** = **went**

Some stay the same. Examples: **beat** = **beat**, **put** = **put**

Osiris, God of Transition, is shown with green skin, to remind people of the fields that grow after the floods.

Mice cause such a problem in Egypt that cats have their own goddess, Bastet.

Geb, God of the Earth, wears a goose on his head.

Ancient Egyptians believe the earth shakes whenever Geb laughs.

Ancient Egyptians don't celebrate the New Year on any particular date, but hold gatherings and feasts whenever the floods come.

Irregular Verbs

Upon completion, add these stickers to your path on the map!

BONUS: What are the past-tense forms of the following verbs: is, become, bind, take?

Now add this sticker to your map!

22

The Richest King

Read about King Mansa Musa.
Then answer each question.

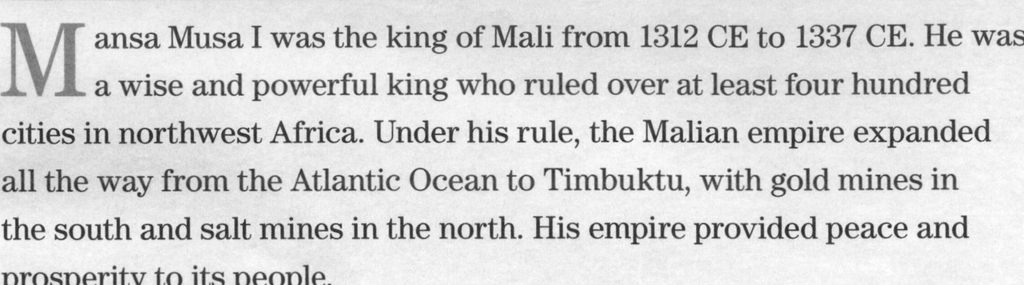

Individuals and Communities

Mansa Musa I was the king of Mali from 1312 CE to 1337 CE. He was a wise and powerful king who ruled over at least four hundred cities in northwest Africa. Under his rule, the Malian empire expanded all the way from the Atlantic Ocean to Timbuktu, with gold mines in the south and salt mines in the north. His empire provided peace and prosperity to its people.

Mansa Musa may have been the richest man who ever lived, with a fortune possibly worth $400 billion today. But he wasn't only interested in treasure. He paid architects and scholars to build palaces, cities, and places of worship that were enjoyed for generations. He was also a patron of learning and the arts. He used his riches to create a great university in Timbuktu, which made the city an important center of education in Africa for years to come. That university still stands today.

Upon completion, add this sticker to your path on the map!

How did the size of the Malian empire change during Mansa Musa's life?

___

What might life have been like for the people of Mali while Mansa Musa was king?

___

What are four things that Mansa Musa spent his treasure on?

___

Was education important to Mansa Musa? How do you know?

___

___

How did Mansa Musa's decisions affect people's lives after he was gone?

___

___

Brain Box

An **inference** is a logical conclusion. You can make an inference by combining what you already know with new information, and then thinking about a reasonable result.

Objects in Motion

Read about kinetic energy.

When an object is in motion, it has **kinetic energy**. An object's kinetic energy, or movement energy, depends on its mass (a measure of how much matter is in an object) and its speed (a measure of how fast it's going). Objects that are moving fast have worked to accelerate, or speed up, and will need to perform the same amount of work to slow down again.

Indeed, the **first law of motion** states just that—an object in motion tends to stay in motion—unless something stops it. Isaac Newton developed this theory of physics in 1687, as he investigated objects and how they moved. He noticed that objects with a large mass are harder to move initially, but also harder to stop once they are moving. Objects with a smaller mass can accelerate with less work and also require less work to slow down.

Upon completion, add this sticker to your path on the map!

Look at the drawings of objects and answer each question.

Which wagon will be harder to stop and why?

___

___

___

Which flying rock will be harder to stop and why?

___

___

___

When a player shoots one marble at another, what will happen to the shooter's marble? What will happen to the marble that was hit?

___

___

___

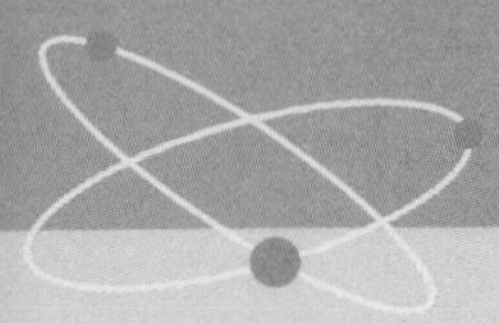

What's Your Wish?

Multiplication: Arrays

Look at each array. Then fill in the factors and find each product.

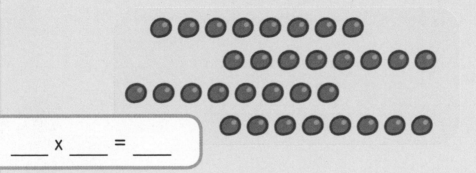

____ x ____ = ____

____ x ____ = ____

____ x ____ = ____

____ x ____ = ____

____ x ____ = ____

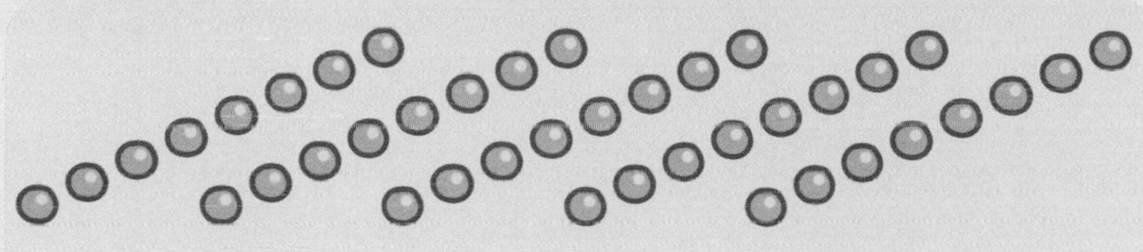

____ x ____ = ____

____ x ____ = ____

____ x ____ = ____

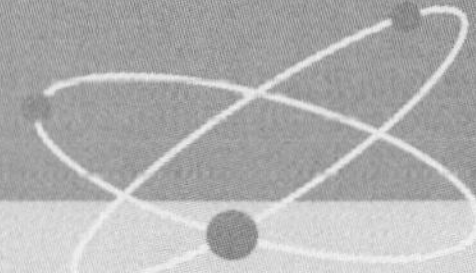

Multiplication: Arrays

Upon completion, add these stickers to your path on the map!

BONUS: The genie will grant you 12 of any object. Choose an object. Then draw 2 arrays that show 2 different ways you can arrange your 12 objects. Write a multiplication equation for each.

____ x ____ = ____

____ x ____ = ____

Now add this sticker to your map!

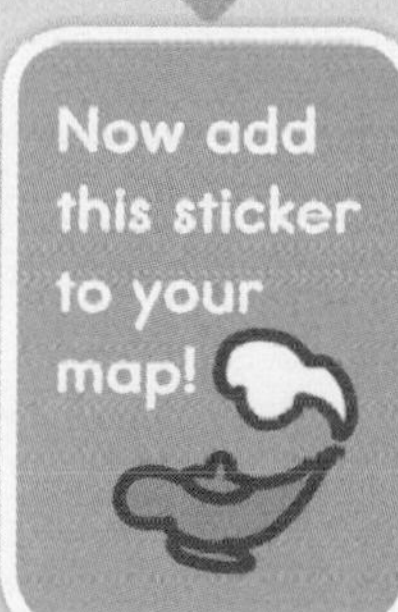

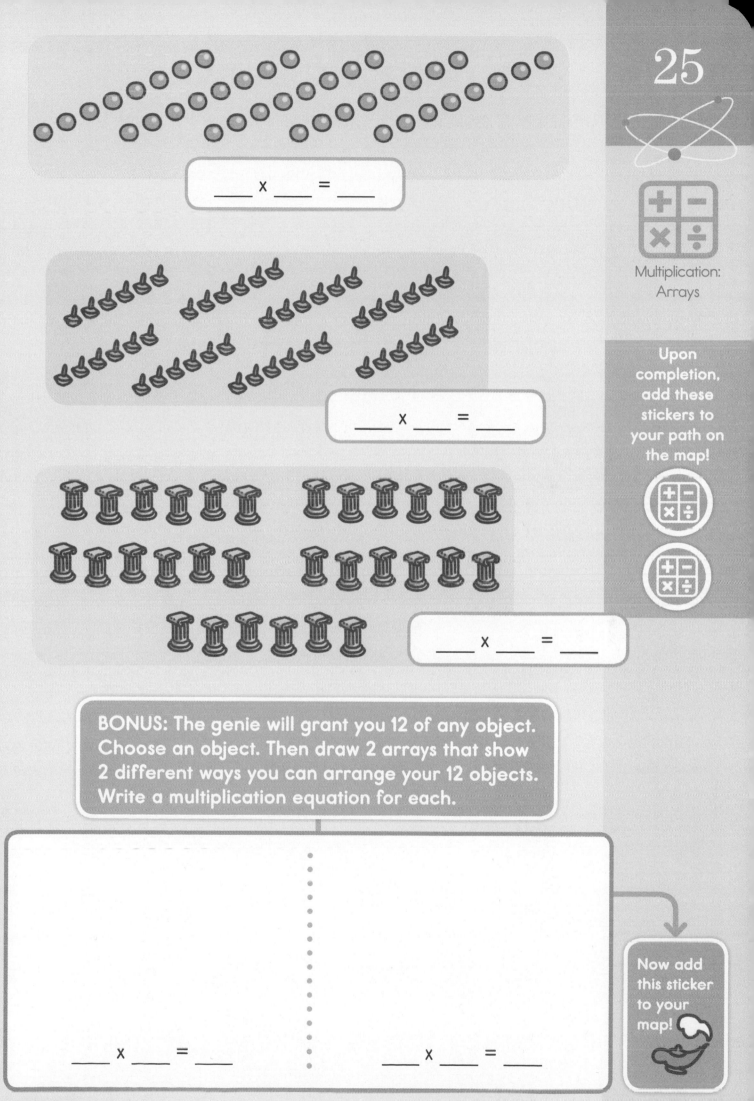

26

Pyramid Mystery

Fill in the blanks with the correct verb tense of each highlighted verb to learn about the Egyptian pyramids.

Verb Tenses

The Egyptian pyramids were ________________ (**construct**) by huge numbers of people—maybe as many as 100,000 people per pyramid. Whole villages ________ (**grow**) up around the construction sites. Builders ________ (**build**), but cooks also ________ (**cook**), and bakers ________ (**bake**) for all the laborers. Pharaohs (Egyptian kings) built the most famous pyramids during the course of about 100 years, between 2630 BCE and 2530 BCE. To provide building blocks workers had to ________ (**mined**) large rocks from quarries with copper tools. How did workers ________ (**got**) them into place? Some rocks ________ (**are**) pushed or pulled. But new research shows that some of the pyramid blocks were made from concrete—so they could have been ________ (**mix**) right there, not ________ (**drag**) all the way from a quarry.

Upon completion, add this sticker to your path on the map!

Point of View

Read the Ghanaian folktale about Anansi the spider. Then answer each question.

Yesterday, I was just sitting down for a delicious lunch when my friend Turtle showed up and eyed my sweet-smelling food. I knew that I should share with my friend, but as the scents wafted up to my nose, my stomach grumbled with hunger and I wanted it all for myself. I had an idea.

"You're welcome to share my lunch," I said. "But your hands are dirty. You had better wash them before you sit down."

As soon as Turtle turned around to head to the river and wash his hands, I gulped down the entire plate of food. When Turtle returned, he surveyed the empty plate. "Don't worry," Turtle said to me. "Tomorrow I will make you lunch so we can eat together." I do love a good meal.

The next day, I went to Turtle's home at the river and peered down. I could see a fine table set on the sand underwater. I filled the pockets of my jacket with rocks from the bank of the river and waded in. With the added weight I sank right down to the table. Turtle greeted me with a frown. "I'm sorry," he said. "It's not polite to wear a jacket at the table."

I was eager to eat, so I agreed to take off my jacket. As I peeled it off, I started to rise! The jacket, and the rocks, stayed down by the food while I floated to the surface of the river. I peered down. There was Turtle, eating the whole meal by himself.

Multiple Perspectives

Upon completion, add this sticker to your path on the map!

Why did Anansi send Turtle to wash his hands?

____

How do you think Turtle felt when he saw that Anansi had eaten all the lunch?

____

____

From Anansi's point of view, was he being a good friend to Turtle? Why or why not?

____

____

How do you think Anansi felt when he saw Turtle eating the whole lunch?

____

____

Brain Box

Different characters have different **points of view**. That means they see the world differently from one another. Point of view can affect how a story is told and what information is included or excluded.

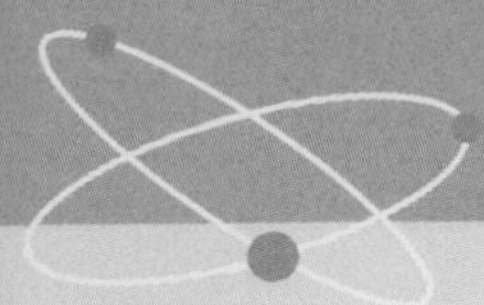

Division

Share the Wealth

The queen is sharing gems among her loyal subjects. How many gems does each subject get? Draw gems in each box to find the quotient. Then complete the division equation.

32 diamonds shared equally among 4 subjects:

___ ÷ ___ = ___

20 rubies shared equally among 5 subjects:

___ ÷ ___ = ___

21 pearls shared equally among 3 subjects:

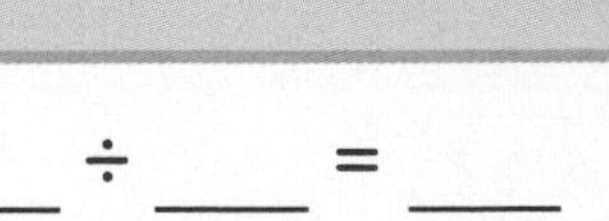

___ ÷ ___ = ___

18 emeralds shared equally between 2 subjects:

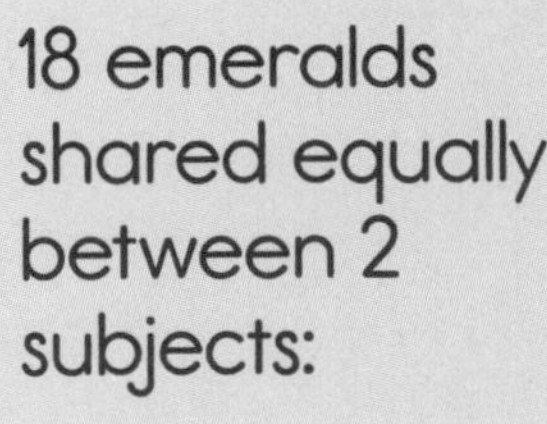

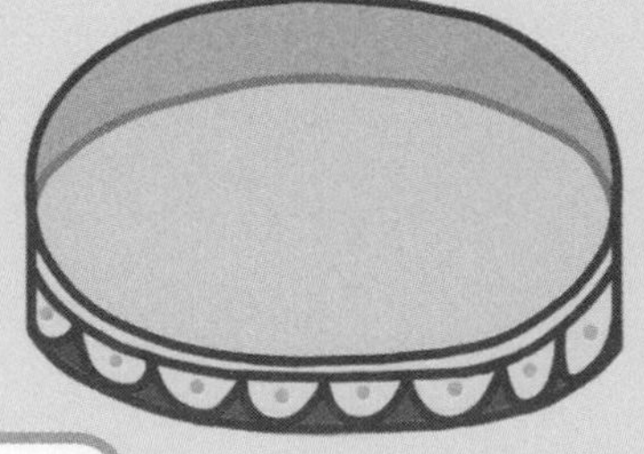

___ ÷ ___ = ___

Upon completion, add this sticker to your path on the map!

Brain Box

When you **divide**, you share a number of items or split them into equal groups and find out how many are in each group.

You divide a **dividend** by a **divisor** to get a **quotient**.

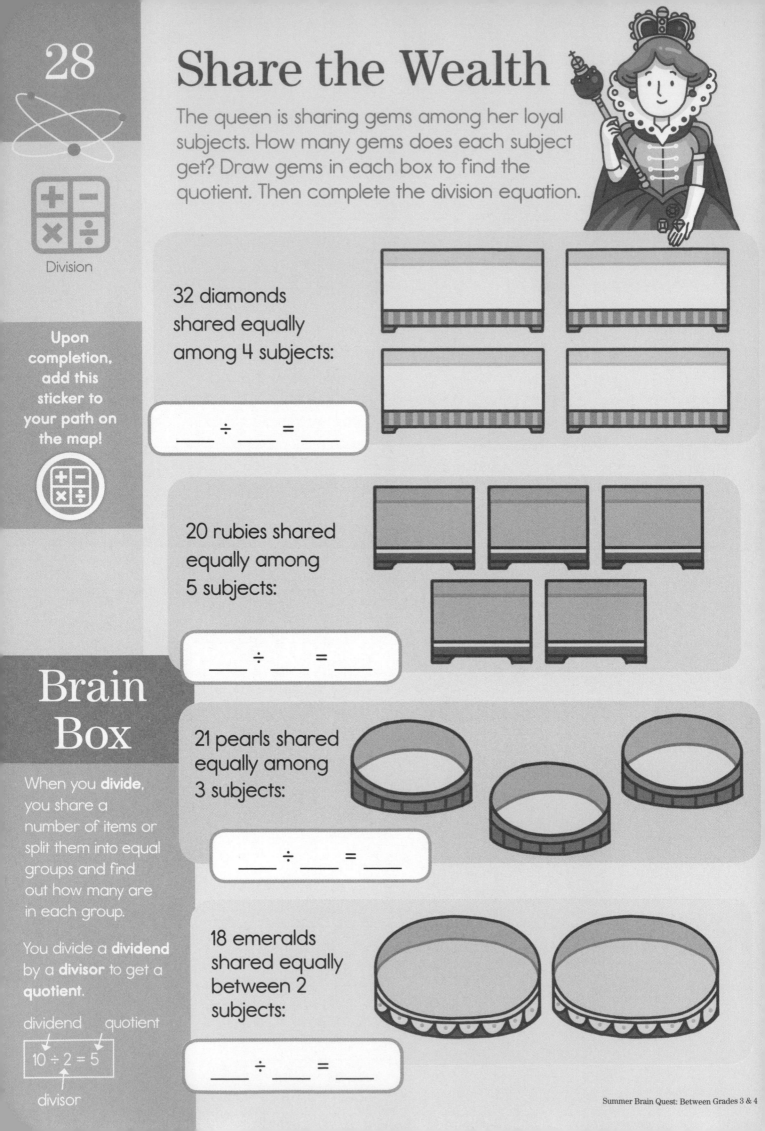

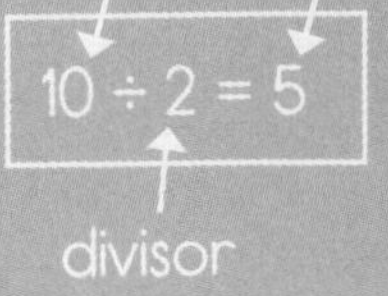

Add this achievement sticker to your path…

…and move on to

Level 3A

on page 30!

…or move on to

Level 3B

on page 44!

30

How to Name a City

Read the story. Then answer each question using complete sentences.

Main Idea and Supporting Details

START LEVEL 3A HERE!

Athena vs. Poseidon

Once there was a beautiful city by the sea. It was so beautiful that Athena, the goddess of wisdom, and Poseidon, the god of the sea, got into an argument over it. They both wanted to be the one to protect and defend it.

To settle the argument peacefully, they decided to ask the people of the city.

When all the people came to meet Poseidon and Athena, Poseidon struck the ground with his trident. Water spurted out!

The residents were delighted until they tasted it. Because Poseidon was god of the sea, it was seawater—no good for drinking, or washing, or watering plants! What a disappointment!

Then Athena stuck her spear in the ground. Where she did, a beautiful olive tree grew up! It had beautiful wood and was full of fruits that were good for eating and making oil.

Now the people were overjoyed. They chose Athena as their defender and named the city after her: Athens.

Brain Box

A **main idea** is the key message of a story; it's explained and reinforced by **supporting details** from the text.

What did Poseidon offer the people?

____

What did Athena offer the people?

____

What are three reasons why Poseidon's gift wasn't good for the city?

____

____

____

What three things did Athena's gift have to offer the people of Athens?

____

____

____

Is the main idea of the story that Poseidon is a bad gift giver or that Athena gave the better gift? Find evidence in the passage to support your answer.

____

____

____

Why was Athena's gift the better gift? Include supporting details from the text in your answer.

____

____

____

Main Idea and Supporting Details

Upon completion, add this sticker to your path on the map!

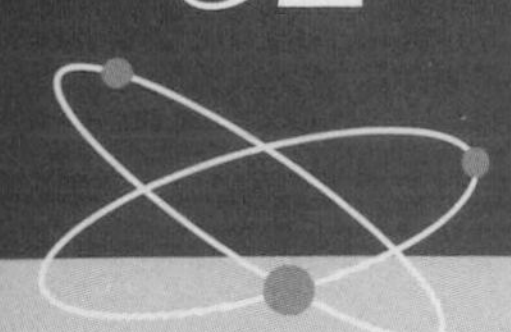

Read the Signs

Look at the hieroglyphics. Then fill in the blanks with a preposition or a prepositional phrase that describes where each symbol is located.

Prepositional Phrases

The bird is ____________ the throne.

The snake is ____________ the crown.

The horse is ____________ the chariot.

The lion is ____________ the queen.

The cat is ____________ the lion.

Upon completion, add this sticker to your path on the map!

Brain Box

A **preposition** shows how nouns and pronouns relate to other words in a sentence. A preposition usually shows **where** something is or **when** something happened. For example: The dragon flew **over** the mountainside.

What's the Point?

Read the ancient Greek proverbs that each person has chosen. Then circle the best conclusion you can reach about each person based on what you have read.

Drawing Conclusions

Alex's Proverbs

A library is full of medicine for the mind.

Wonder is the beginning of wisdom.

Conclusions

- Alex likes to read and learn new things.
- Alex is sick and takes medicine.
- Alex wants to go to the library.

Chloe's Proverbs

Better late than never.

Better five in your hand than ten somewhere else.

Conclusions

- Chloe knows that it's OK to run late if you are coming from somewhere else.
- Chloe thinks that it's important to not be late when paying a debt.
- Chloe would rather have an imperfect version of something than risk having nothing at all.

Upon completion, add this sticker to your path on the map!

Daphne's Proverbs

The pen is mightier than the sword.

The tongue has no bones, but it breaks bones.

Conclusions

- Daphne has a sharp pen and sword.
- Daphne knows that words can hurt people's feelings.
- Daphne thinks that swords break bones.

Brain Box

A **conclusion** is the most likely outcome that you arrive at based on reasons and evidence.

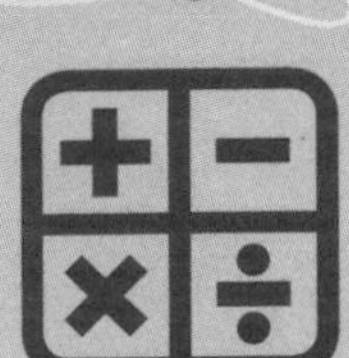

Division

Chariot Pit Stop

How many chariots can the Romans make? Draw circles around an equal number of wheels to find the quotient. Then complete the division equation.

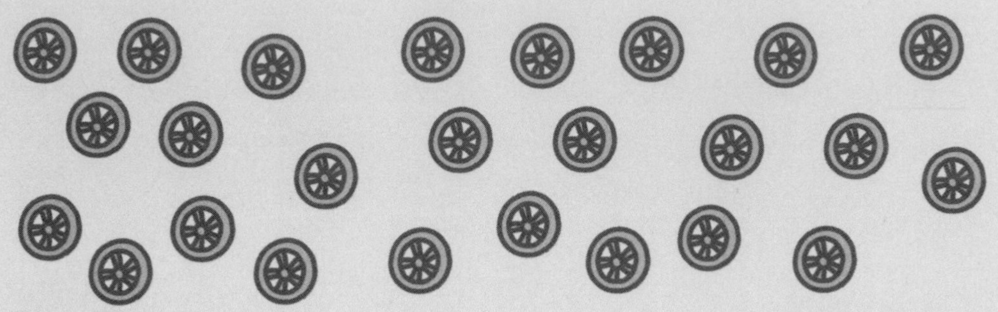

There are 25 wheels. Each chariot needs 5 wheels.

____ ÷ ____ = ____ chariots

There are 16 wheels. Each chariot needs 8 wheels.

____ ÷ ____ = ____ chariots

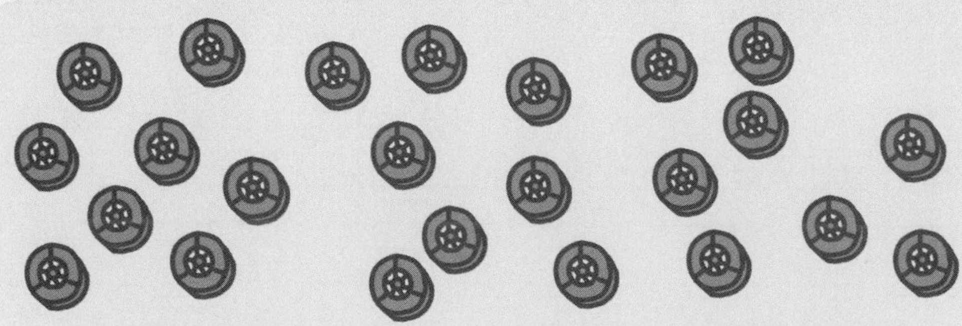

There are 24 wheels. Each chariot needs 8 wheels.

____ ÷ ____ = ____ chariots

How many chariots were made in all?

____ + ____ + ____ = ____ chariots

Upon completion, add this sticker to your path on the map!

Preparing for the Worst

Read the passage. Then look at each picture below, and write the matching bold word or phrase about preparations for the severe weather.

Weather Hazards

Severe weather can cause severe problems. Hard rain can cause rivers to overflow and flood nearby cities. High winds can damage buildings and crops. Extreme temperatures can cause fires and endanger the lives of people, animals, and plants. But people can also prepare for bad weather and prevent some of its effects. **Lightning rods** can harness and direct the power of lightning strikes. **Sandbags** piled on riverbanks can raise the banks and keep nearby communities safe from rising waters. **Hedges and windbreaks** can protect crops and yards from high winds. Buildings can also be built with weather-resistant features that make them better able to withstand extreme temperatures and harsh storms.

Rising floodwaters in the Nile River

____

A windstorm on farmland

____

A thunderstorm

____

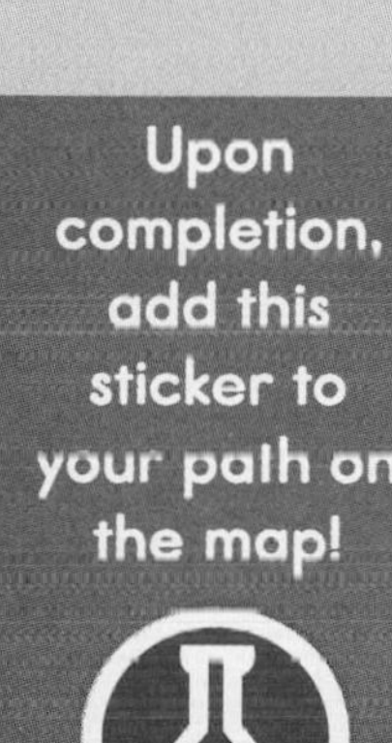

Upon completion, add this sticker to your path on the map!

BONUS: How might a chariot driver prepare his chariot for a flood?

____

____

____

Now add this sticker to your map!

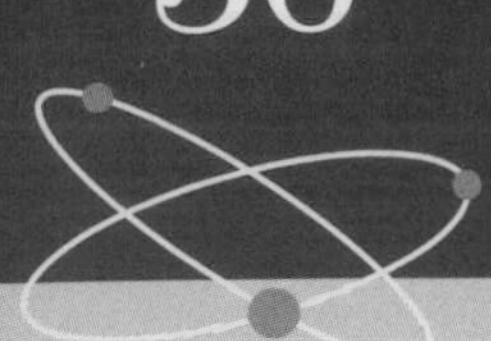

Time in Troy

Chronology and Timelines

Study the events on the timeline. Then number the scenes of the story in the correct order.

Seeing the Greeks sail away and thinking they'd won, the Trojans began to celebrate the end of the long war. Feeling victorious, they brought their gift horse inside their city.

But the hollow belly of the horse didn't stay empty for long. When the horse was finished, many of the Greeks' strongest fighters hid inside.

1 For many years, Greece and Troy were at war. The whole Greek army was camped outside Troy's city gates. But no matter what they did, the Greeks couldn't get into the city.

Then, the remaining Greek soldiers left the filled horse outside the city gates of Troy as a "gift," got into their boats, and pretended to sail away.

But after the Trojans brought the wooden horse inside the city gates, they got a big surprise. That night, when all the Trojans were tired from celebrating, the Greeks climbed out, took over the city, and won the war!

Because the Greeks couldn't fight their way in, they came up with another plan. They would trick the Trojans into opening the gates. So they built a giant wooden horse with a hollow belly.

Chronology and Timelines

Upon completion, add these stickers to your path on the map!

38

Monster Multiplication

Write an equation to solve each word problem.

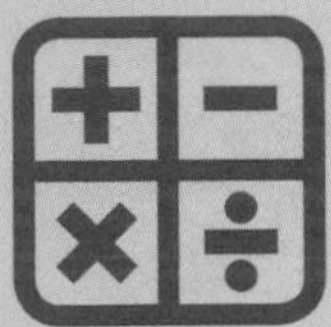

Multiplication: Word Problems

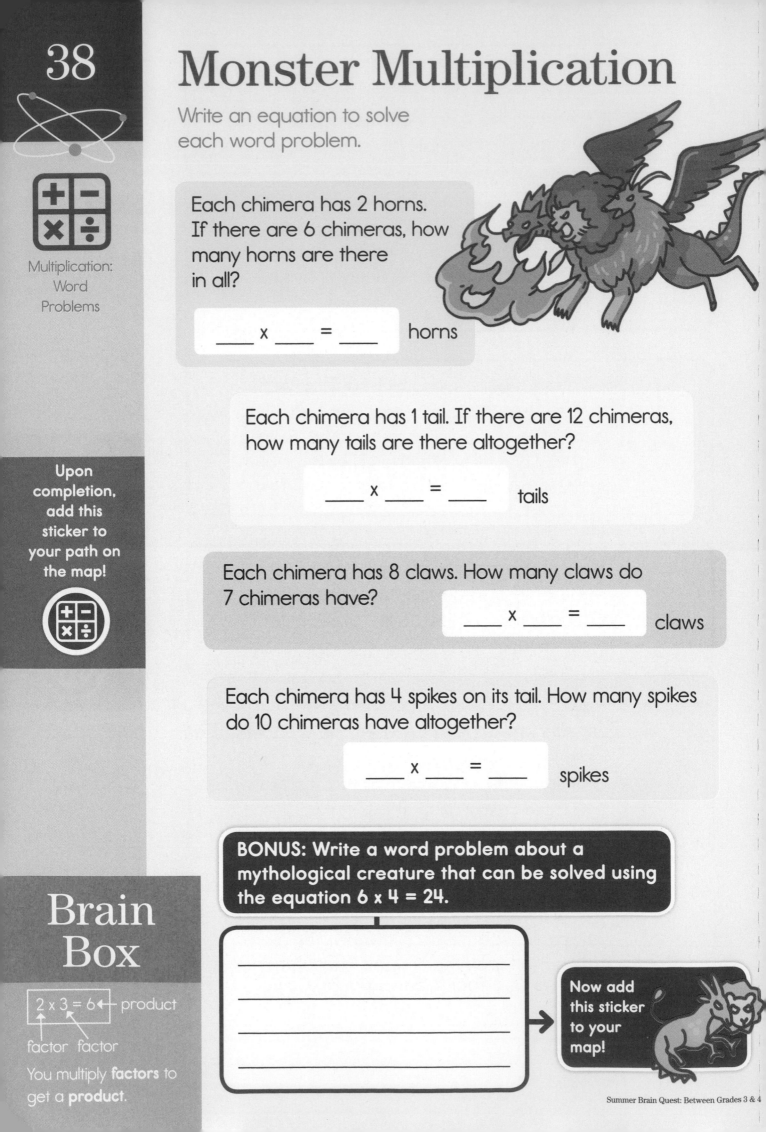

Each chimera has 2 horns. If there are 6 chimeras, how many horns are there in all?

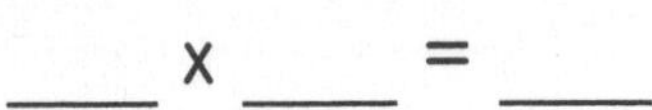

____ x ____ = ____ horns

Each chimera has 1 tail. If there are 12 chimeras, how many tails are there altogether?

____ x ____ = ____ tails

Upon completion, add this sticker to your path on the map!

Each chimera has 8 claws. How many claws do 7 chimeras have?

____ x ____ = ____ claws

Each chimera has 4 spikes on its tail. How many spikes do 10 chimeras have altogether?

____ x ____ = ____ spikes

BONUS: Write a word problem about a mythological creature that can be solved using the equation 6 x 4 = 24.

____

____

____

____

Now add this sticker to your map!

Brain Box

2 x 3 = 6 ← product

factor factor

You multiply **factors** to get a **product**.

Sunny Seasons

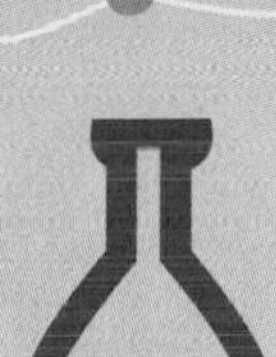

Seasons

Read the text. Then answer each question.

All of the planets in the solar system orbit the sun, including Earth. Earth takes 365.26 days to complete its orbit around the sun, which is how we measure one Earth year.

Earth also rotates on its axis at the same time. It takes Earth 24 hours to make one full rotation on its axis, which is how we measure one Earth day. Earth's axis is also tilted, so different parts of the planet lean toward the warm sun at different times of the year. The direction of the tilt toward or away from the sun causes the four seasons: winter, spring, summer, and fall.

Earth is divided into sections called hemispheres. Using the equator as a divider, the Northern Hemisphere is the land and water to the north, while the Southern Hemisphere is the area to the south. Summer occurs in the one hemisphere that is closest to the sun's light and heat. Winter occurs in the one hemisphere that is farthest from the sun. So, while it is summer in the Northern Hemisphere, it is winter in the Southern Hemisphere!

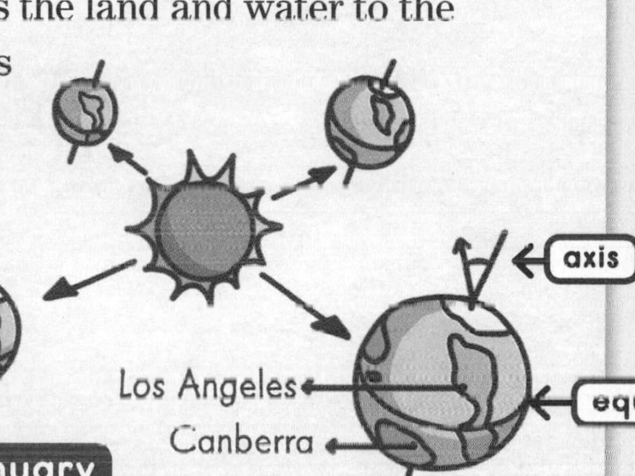

Upon completion, add this sticker to your path on the map!

Mars takes 687 days to orbit the sun. How long is a year on Mars?

____

What is the season in Los Angeles, California, in January, and why?

____

____

What is the season in Canberra, Australia, in January, and why?

____

____

How does the earth's tilt affect the seasons?

____

____

40

Finding Your Way

Look at the map of ancient Troy. Then answer each question.

Direction and Distance

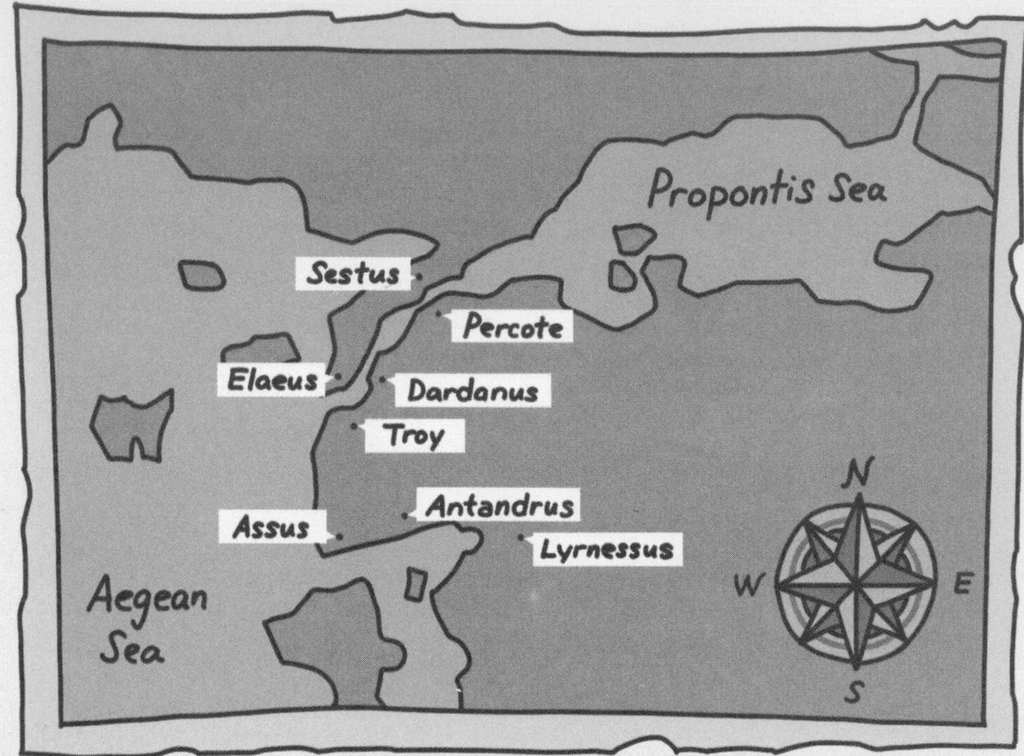

Upon completion, add this sticker to your path on the map!

To reach Elaeus from Troy, which direction must you travel?

____

From Troy, is it farther to reach Dardanus or Antandrus?

____

Which cities require crossing the water to reach them from Troy?

____

Which city is north of Percote? _______________

Which journey would take longer—traveling from Sestus to Elaeus, or from Troy to Lyrnessus?

____

BONUS: If Troy existed today, in what country would it be located?

____

Now add this sticker to your map!

Which Works?

Fill in the relative pronoun or relative adverb to complete the story.

that whose when

where who why whom

Now is the moment __________ we need a hero, but __________ can help us? You may wonder __________ we need help. Because only a brave warrior can save our city from the sea monster! It must be someone __________ bravery is unquestionable. It must be someone for __________ no challenge is too hard. It wouldn't hurt if she or he had a shield __________ could turn an enemy to stone. If someone will rescue us, our city will be the home __________ she or he can live forever.

41

Relative Pronouns and Relative Adverbs

Upon completion, add this sticker to your path on the map!

Brain Box

A **relative pronoun**, such as who, whom, whose, that, and which, relates to another noun or pronoun in a sentence. A **relative adverb**, such as where, when, and why, is an adverb that introduces a **relative clause**, a dependent clause that functions like an adjective.

Knights Divided

Solve each word problem. Write an equation and the quotient.

Division: Word Problems

Upon completion, add this sticker to your path on the map!

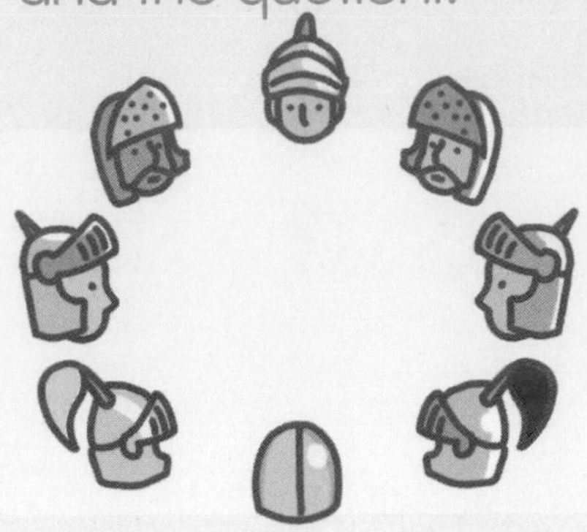

40 knights sit at round tables. If each table fits 8 knights, how many tables are there?

___ ÷ ___ = ___ tables

If a knight has 48 arrows and uses 6 arrows in each battle, how many battles can he fight before he runs out of arrows?

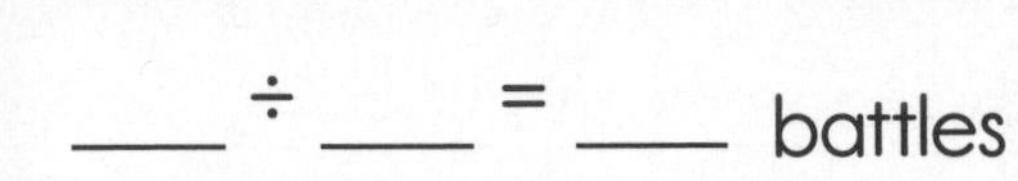

___ ÷ ___ = ___ battles

If a group of 42 knights on horseback lines up in rows of 6 knights, how many rows of knights are there?

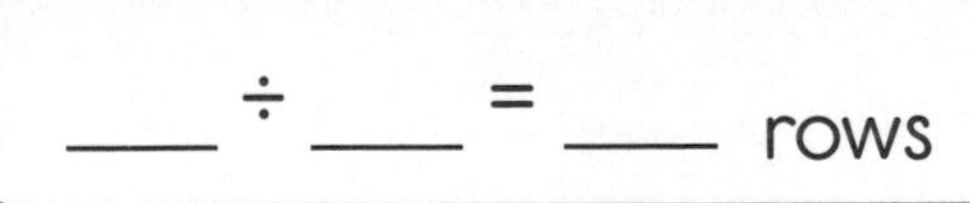

___ ÷ ___ = ___ rows

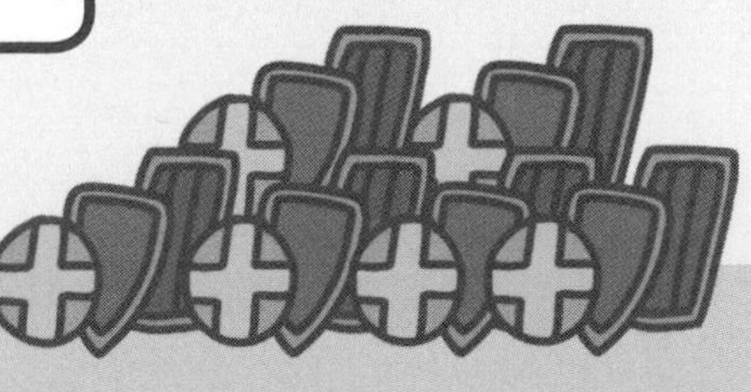

Each knight owns 2 shields. There are 18 shields in the castle shed. How many knights are inside the castle?

___ ÷ ___ = ___ knights

A spy peeks into the stable and counts 28 horse legs. How many horses are in the stable?

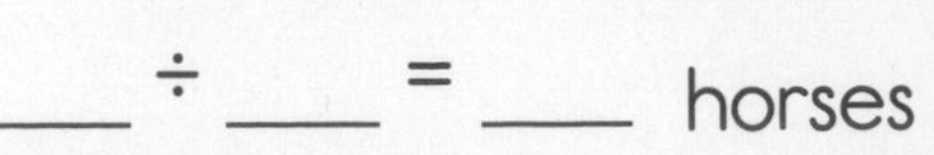

___ ÷ ___ = ___ horses

Level 3A complete!

Add this achievement sticker to your path...

...and move on to

Level 4A

on page 58...

...OR GO ON AN OUTSIDE QUEST AND MOVE ON TO LEVEL 4B ON PAGE 68!

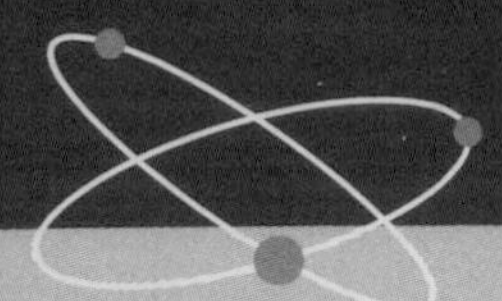

Multiplying Dragons

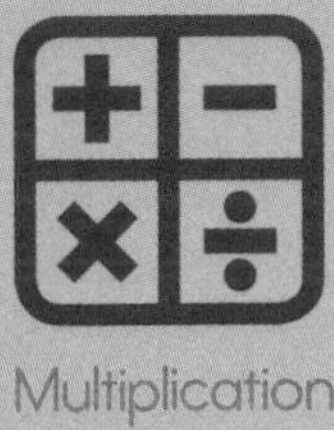

Multiplication Properties

START LEVEL 3B HERE!

Fill in the blanks to find each product. Then write the multiplication property each problem demonstrates.

5 x 2 = ____

So 2 x ____ = ____

____ property

3 x 4 x 2 = (3 x 4) x ____

= ____ x 2

= ____

____ property

9 x 6 = ____

So 6 x ____ = ____

____ property

Upon completion, add these stickers to your path on the map!

Brain Box

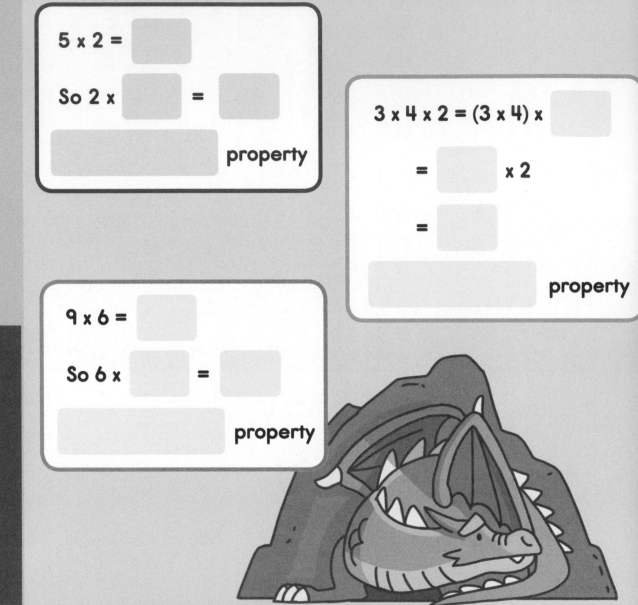

The **Commutative Property** says you can multiply in any order and the product will be the same.
3 x 4 = 12 and 4 x 3 = 12

The **Associative Property** says you can group factors in any way and the product will be the same.
2 x 3 x 4 can be found by 2 x 3 = 6 and 6 x 4 = 24 or 3 x 4 = 12 and 2 x 12 = 24.

The **Distributive Property** says that multiplying a number by a sum is the same as multiplying the number by each addend and then adding the two products.
2 x (3 + 5) = 2 x 3 + 2 x 5 = 6 + 10 = 16

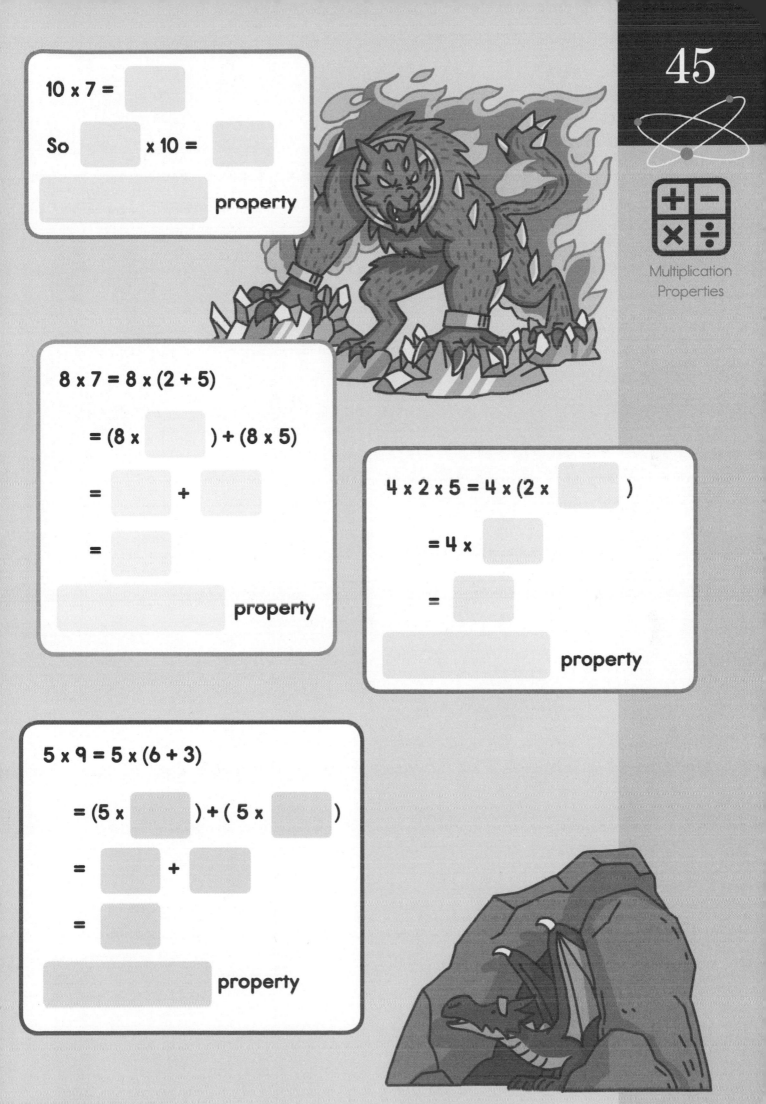

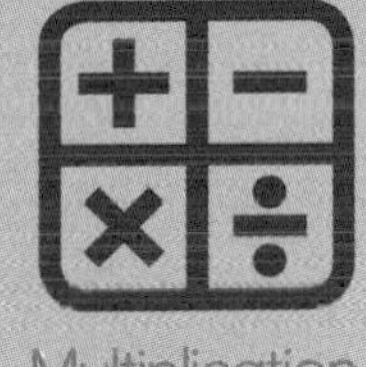

Multiplication Properties

10 x 7 = ______

So ______ x 10 = ______

______ property

8 x 7 = 8 x (2 + 5)

= (8 x ______) + (8 x 5)

= ______ + ______

= ______

______ property

4 x 2 x 5 = 4 x (2 x ______)

= 4 x ______

= ______

______ property

5 x 9 = 5 x (6 + 3)

= (5 x ______) + (5 x ______)

= ______ + ______

= ______

______ property

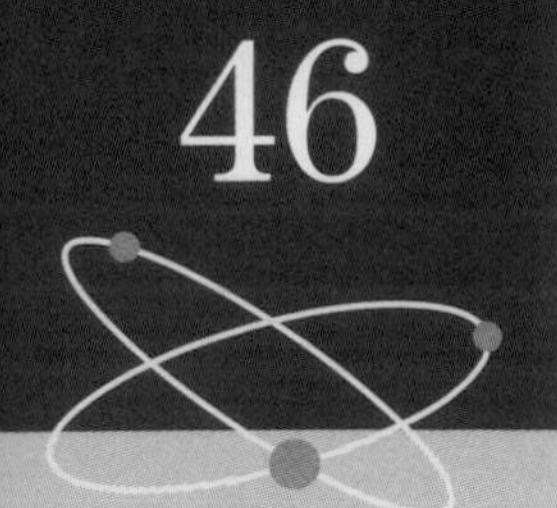

Mysteries in History

Draw a line to match each fossil with its environment.

Fossils and Environment

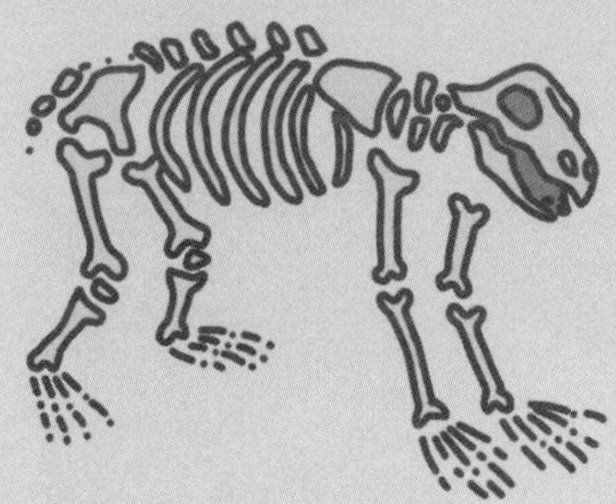

A prehistoric ocean, in which large mammals, smaller fish, and plant life made up a diverse ecosystem.

A primeval forest, in which tall trees shaded the smaller shrubs and plants of the forest floor. Its wildlife included primates, and birds lived in the branches above.

Upon completion, add this sticker to your path on the map!

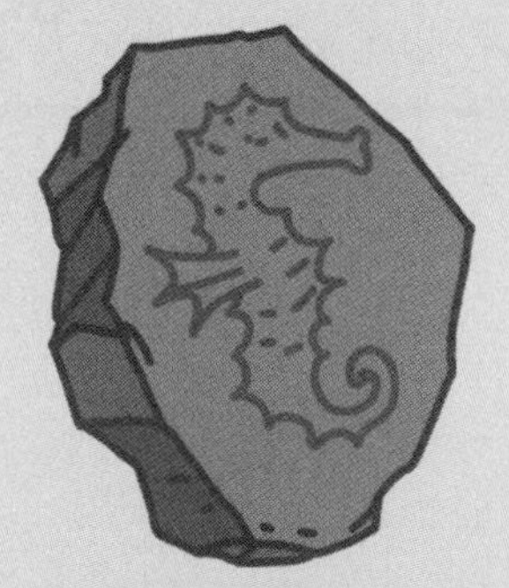

Ancient grasslands, free of large trees, but with a diversity of flowers and grasses, as well as insects and mammals that subsisted on them.

An arctic region millions of years ago. There was a snowy island with ice and large creatures like the Coryphodon and polar bears.

The Silk Road

Read about the Silk Road. Then answer each question.

Trade

The Silk Road is one of the most famous trade routes in history. It stretched from China all the way to Europe, about 4,000 miles. People traveled on it, trading goods from around 114 BCE to 1450 CE. The trade route got its name from Chinese silk, which was in high demand all over the world. For many years, only the Chinese knew how to make it. Indian traders traveled the route with Roman gold and traded with the Chinese to bring the silk to Rome. Travelers also traded tea, sugar, salt, spices, and porcelain. Meanwhile, languages and diseases also spread along the Silk Road. It remained the world's most important trade route until new direct sea routes to Asia were discovered during the Age of Exploration in the fifteenth century.

Upon completion, add this sticker to your path on the map!

What country created the silk that gave the Silk Road its name?

___

What country was so eager for Chinese silk that they sent Indian traders to acquire it?

___

What other goods were carried on the Silk Road?

___

What were two things that spread along the Silk Road, but were not sold?

___

When did the Silk Road become less important? Why?

___

___

___

___

___

Which Wolf?

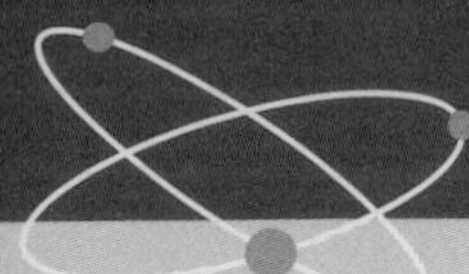

Complete the sentences of the legend from Cherokee folklore by circling the correct highlighted word.

Subject-Verb and Pronoun-Object Agreement

"What happened today?" the grandfather **asked** **ask** his grandson.

"I went to town," the boy told **him** **them** . "Father had furs to trade, and **he** **him** said that because I helped him trap them, I could **get** **got** something for myself."

"Ah!" Grandfather said.

"I looked at all kinds of things, and I finally chose a knife," the boy went on. But instead of looking happy, the boy's face clouded.

"What **happens** **happened** then?" his grandfather asked.

"Father was still trading," the boy said. "So I **gone** **went** outside. And all **them** **these** boys from town started to call me names. They **push** **pushed** me, and I dropped my knife, and **he** **they** picked it up and **run** **ran** away. I hate them!"

His grandfather placed his hand on his grandson's head. "Let me tell you a story," he said. "I **has** **have** felt the same way you do. It's like there are two wolves inside me. One is good, and one is evil. The good wolf **lived** **lives** in harmony with everyone. He only fights when it is right to fight. And he only fights in the right way.

Brain Box

A **legend** is a fictional story handed down from generation to generation. It explains how things came to be or provides reasons for a society's behavior. Every culture has legends, and they are usually told out loud, not written down.

“The evil wolf is always angry. Any little thing will set him off. He’ll fight anyone, at any time, for no good reason. He **have** **has** so much anger that he can’t even think.

“It can be hard to live with both of these wolves fighting inside me,” the grandfather told his grandson.

His grandson stared up into **their** **his** eyes. “Grandfather,” he asked, “which one wins?”

“The one I feed,” his grandfather told him.

Subject-Verb and Pronoun-Object Agreement

Upon completion, add these stickers to your path on the map!

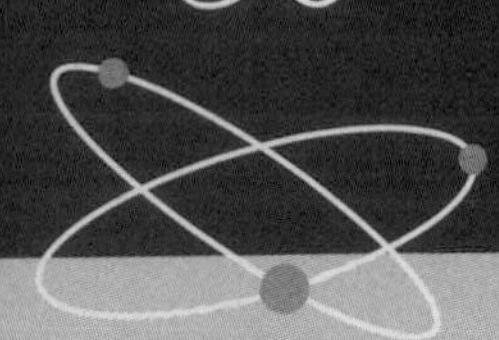

Princess Riddle

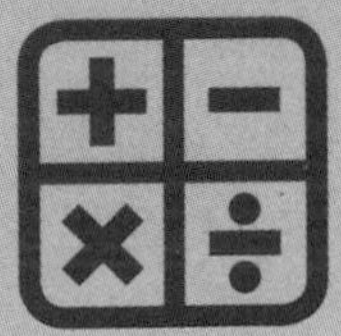

Addition and Subtraction

Find the sums and differences. Use your answers to decode the riddle. (Hint: You may need to regroup.)

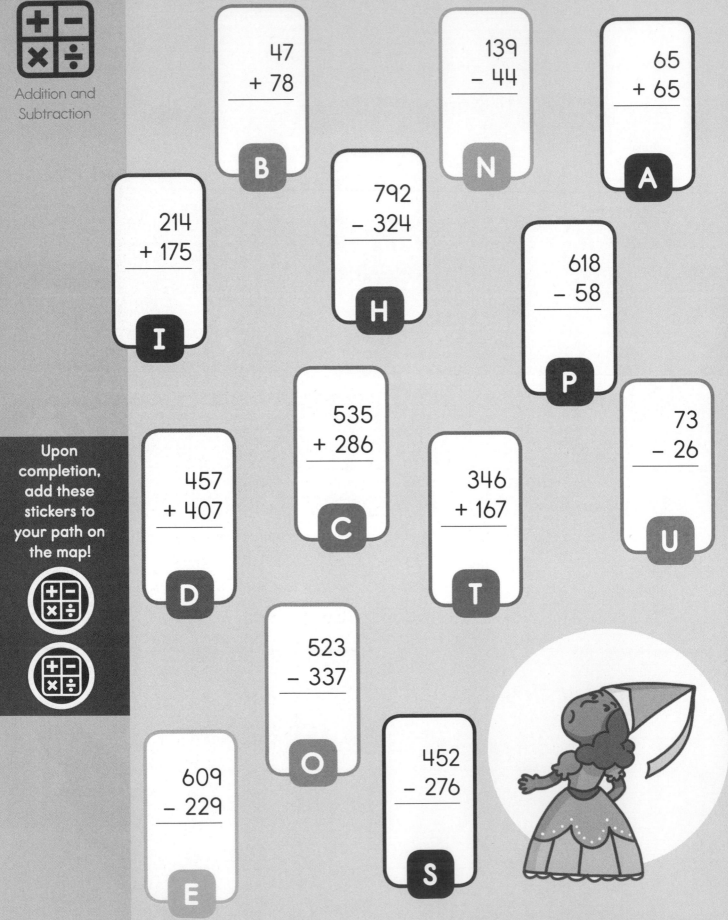

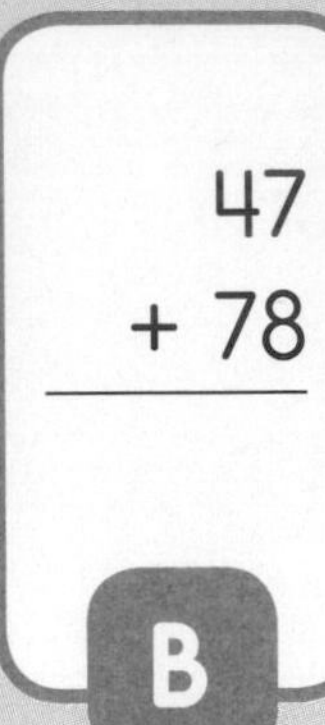

139
− 44

N

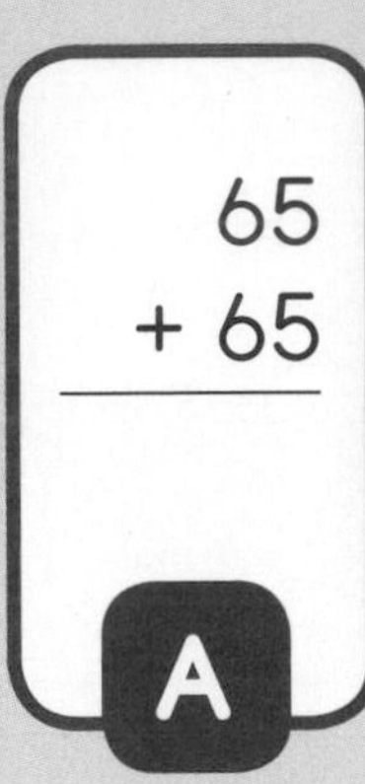

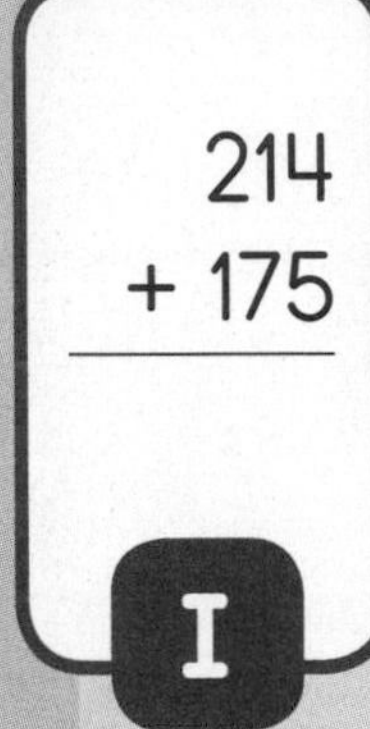

792
− 324

H

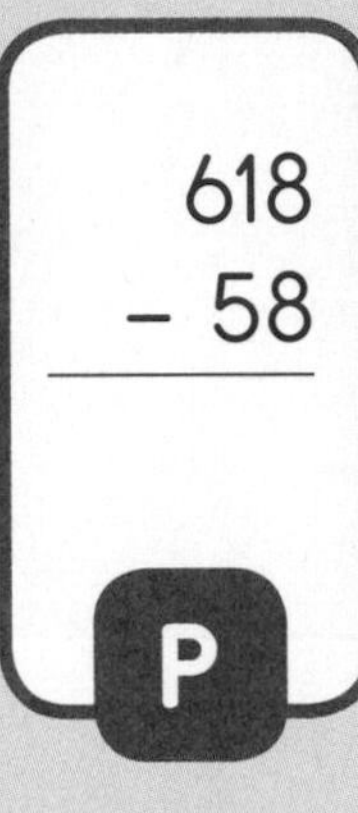

535
+ 286

C

73
− 26

U

457
+ 407

D

346
+ 167

T

Upon completion, add these stickers to your path on the map!

523
− 337

O

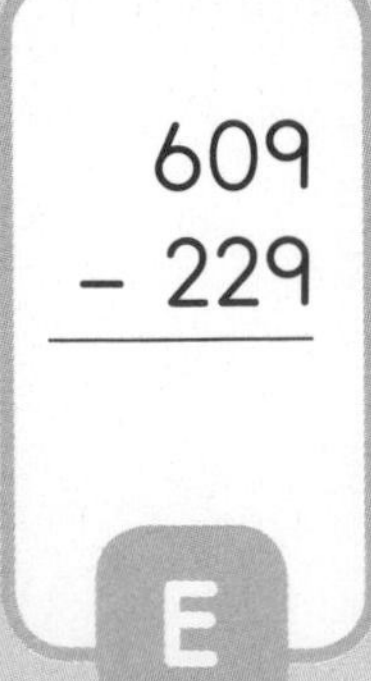

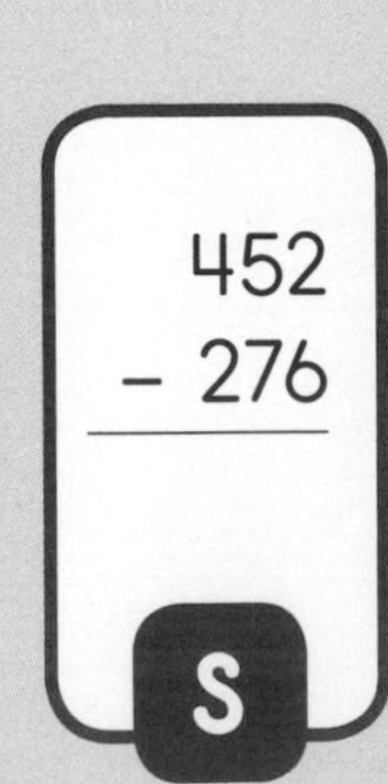

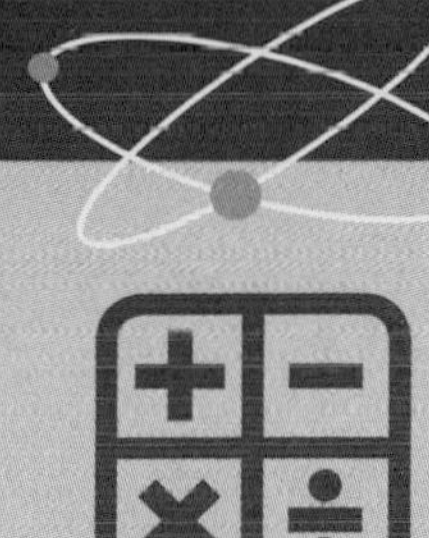

Addition and Subtraction

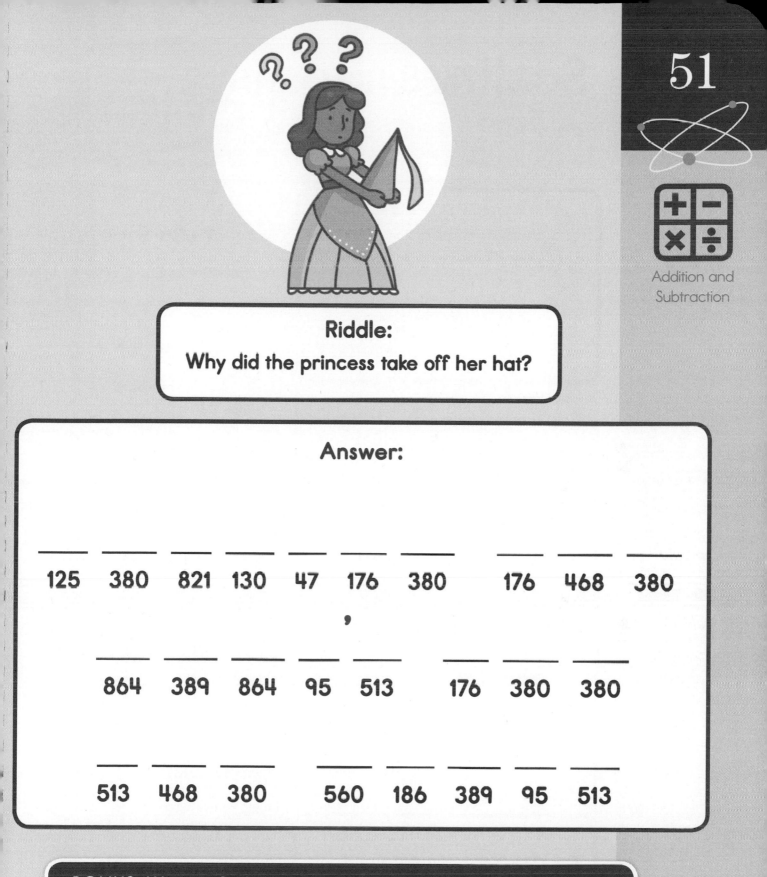

Riddle:
Why did the princess take off her hat?

Answer:

___ ___ ___ ___ ___ ___ ___ ___ ___ ___
125 380 821 130 47 176 380 176 468 380

,

___ ___ ___ ___ ___ ___ ___ ___
864 389 864 95 513 176 380 380

___ ___ ___ ___ ___ ___ ___ ___
513 468 380 560 186 389 95 513

BONUS: Write a 3-digit addition problem and a 3-digit subtraction problem, so that each have the same answer: 513.

Now add this sticker to your map!

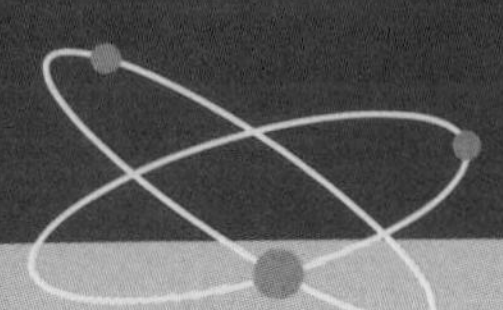

Two-Step Word Problems

Scaling Dragons

Match each problem with its equation by drawing a line. Then solve the problem.

(HINT: n stands for the unknown values.)

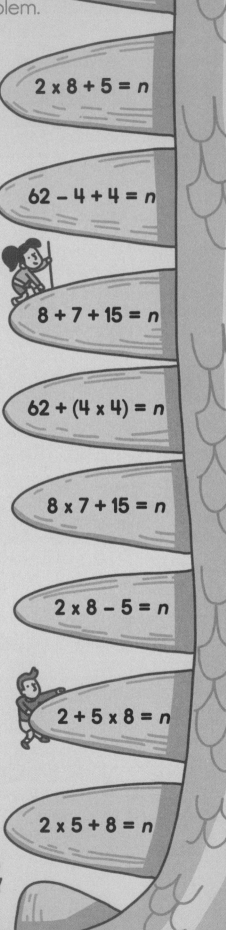

There were 2 groups of explorers with 8 people in each group. If 5 people left after the first day, how many total explorers were left?

____ explorers

The explorers hiked 8 miles a day for 7 days. On the eighth day, they hiked 15 miles. How many miles did they hike in all?

____ miles

4 explorers had a total of 62 liters of water. Then each person added 4 more liters at a well. How many liters of water did they have in all?

____ liters

When the dragon woke up, the explorers ran away for 2 miles. Then they rested, and hiked 5 more miles away each day for 8 days. How many miles away from the dragon did they get?

____ miles

$2 \times 8 + 5 = n$

$62 - 4 + 4 = n$

$8 + 7 + 15 = n$

$62 + (4 \times 4) = n$

$8 \times 7 + 15 = n$

$2 \times 8 - 5 = n$

$2 + 5 \times 8 = n$

$2 \times 5 + 8 = n$

Upon completion, add this sticker to your path on the map!

The Wizard's Apprentices

Comparative and Superlative Adjectives

Upon completion, add this sticker to your path on the map!

Fill in the missing words on the wizard's scroll.

big, __________, biggest

__________, smarter, smartest

fast, faster, __________

dark, __________, darkest

__________, older, oldest

bright, brighter, __________

Remove the suffix of each word, and write the simple adjective. Then write a sentence using both forms of the adjectives.

shorter ______

____

____

quickest ______

____

____

smelliest ______

____

____

Brain Box

When an adjective ends in a **y**, turn the **y** into an **i** before adding **er** or **est**.

Example: **friendly**, **friendlier**, or **friendliest**.

54

Viking Territory

Number the unit squares in each Viking territory. Then write the area of each region.

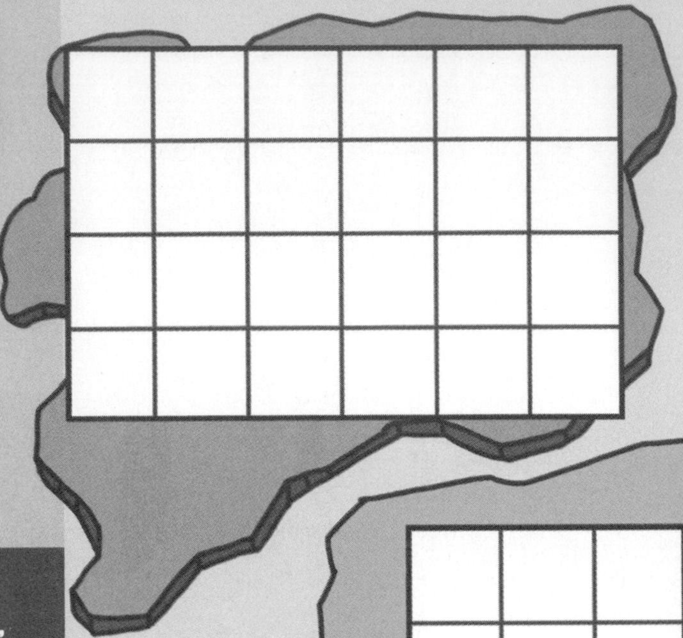

Unit Squares

Area of region is ☐ square units.

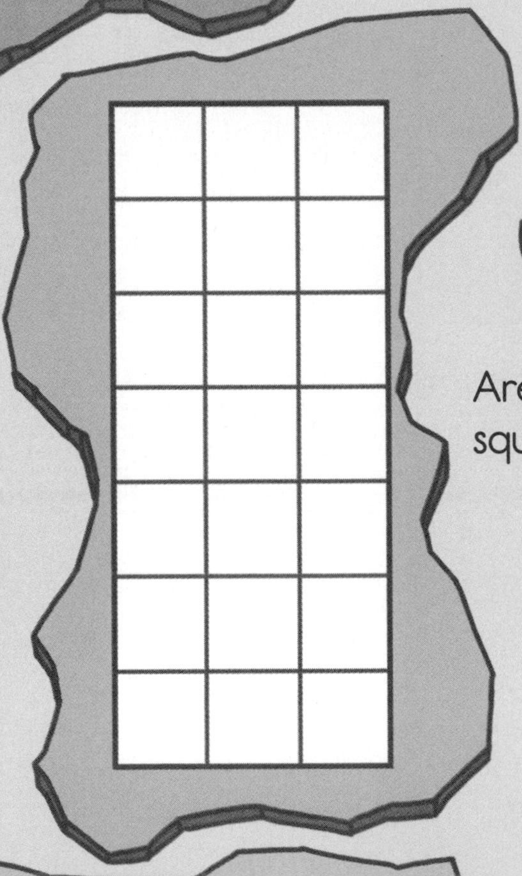

Area of region is ☐ square units.

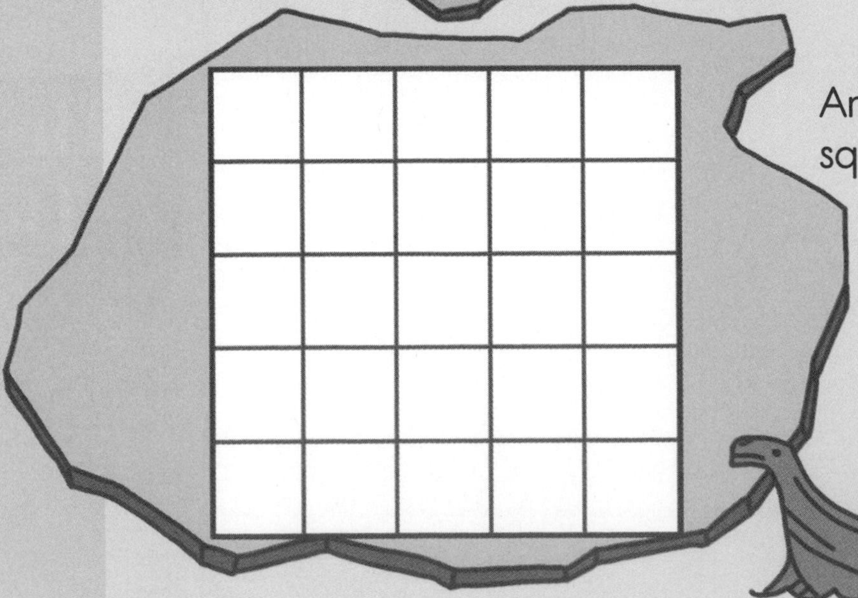

Area of region is ☐ square units.

Upon completion, add this sticker to your path on the map!

Brain Box

The **area** of a figure is the number of **square units** inside a figure.

Adaptation

Animal Adaptation

Look at each animal's adaptation, and write whether it is used for defense, communication, reproduction, or survival (to survive difficult habitats). There may be more than one answer for each.

hard shell

bright throat

warm feathers

water storage

signaling markings

loud song

Upon completion, add this sticker to your path on the map!

BONUS: Why might wolves' teeth be important for survival?

Now add this sticker to your map!

Brain Box

Life-forms usually adapt to defend against predators (attackers), to survive in different habitats (natural environments), to communicate with other animals, or to find a mate and reproduce.

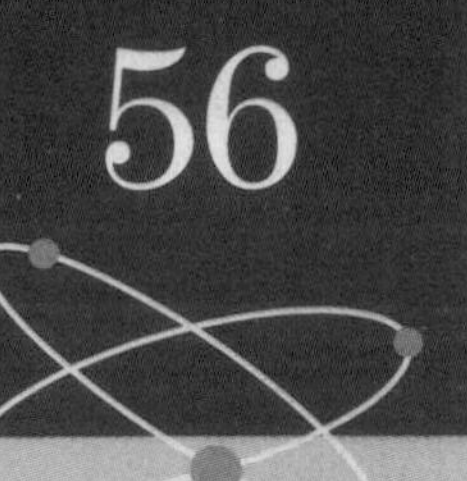

56

The Magic Sword

Fill in the helping verbs to find out how King Arthur became king.

Helping Verbs

England needed a king. Laws were being broken and bandits __________ constantly robbing people. Even the corn that was meant to feed the poor __________ being trampled in the streets.

Legend said that whoever could pull the sword from a great stone in London would be the next king. But nobody could do it. Knights from all over the country ______ come to a tournament to try. They __________ tugging and shouting, but the sword didn't move.

A boy named Arthur came to town with a knight named Ector. Arthur's only job was to take care of Ector's sword. But he lost it! As he __________ running through the city looking for Ector's sword, he found a sword just sticking out of a stone. So he grabbed it and took it to Ector.

Ector couldn't believe it when he recognized the sword. When all the nobles gathered again, Arthur was the only one who could put the sword in the stone and remove it.

One by one, the nobles began to bow before small Arthur. And Arthur __________ named the boy king of England.

Upon completion, add this sticker to your path on the map!

Brain Box

Helping verbs can be used to help tell about an action. They are always used before a verb.

For example: The princess **had** traveled the world. In this example, **had** is the helping verb for the action verb **traveled**, which is in the past tense and shows that the action took place in the past.

Level 3B complete!

Add this achievement sticker to your path...

...AND GO ON AN OUTSIDE QUEST AND MOVE ON TO LEVEL 4A ON PAGE 58!

...or move on to

Level 4B

on page 68!

Carnival!

Read each sentence. Then write whether it is a simple, compound, or complex sentence.

Sentence Structures

Brazil's Carnival in Rio de Janeiro is the biggest carnival in the world.

____

Just before the season of Lent each year, Carnival is celebrated.

____

Although the exact origin of Carnival is unknown, it possibly began in ancient Rome and then spread around the world.

____

In Rio de Janeiro, two million people a day fill the streets, and everyone celebrates.

____

People wear wild costumes in street parades, and they also dress up to go to fancy balls.

____

But no matter where they are, everybody dances.

____

Brain Box

A **simple sentence** has only one independent clause. A **compound sentence** has at least two independent clauses. A **complex sentence** contains an independent clause and one or more subordinate clauses (a clause that is dependent on a main clause).

A **coordinating conjunction**, like **and**, **for**, or **but**, is placed between parts of a sentence that have equal weight. A **subordinating conjunction**, like **because**, **before**, or **when**, introduces a subordinate clause.

Sentence Structures

Read each sentence. Then write whether the highlighted conjunction is coordinating or subordinating.

The classic Carnival dance is a samba, **so** everybody does it.

____

But some sambas are more complicated **than** others.

____

People gather in groups before Carnival **and** prepare special sambas to perform.

____

The streets are also filled with musicians, **because** to dance, people need music.

____

The days of dancing all come to an end on Ash Wednesday, **when** Lent begins.

____

Upon completion, add these stickers to your path on the map!

Centaur Cents

Write why each good is not as easy to trade as money.

Money Exchange

one ton of bronze vs. 20 coins

a year of labor vs. 20 coins

Upon completion, add this sticker to your path on the map!

a parcel of land vs. 20 coins

produce vs. 20 coins

BONUS: If a centaur doll is equal to 10 plums, and each plum costs 9 cents, how much is a centaur doll worth in money?

Now add this sticker to your map!

Gorilla Genes

Read about Cross River gorillas.

Inherited Traits and Variation

Members of the same species, like endangered Cross River gorillas, all share some features. For instance, Cross River gorillas have shorter skulls and smaller hands than other related species of gorillas. Those features are *inherited*, which means that they're passed down through genes from parent to child. But even though all Cross River gorillas share many features, they're not all identical. That's because of *genetic variation*, the individual features or combinations of features that are unique to that one single gorilla. Genetic variations make each gorilla the only one like it in the world.

Look at the gorilla parents and their children. Then write one trait each child inherited from a parent.

Upon completion, add this sticker to your path on the map!

____

____

____

____

Name a trait you inherited and a genetic variation that makes you unique in your family.

____

Brain Box

An **inherited trait** is a trait that is passed down genetically from a parent or grandparent. **Genetic variation** describes the differences between members of a family or species.

Area

An Island of One's Own

Multiply length by width to find the area.

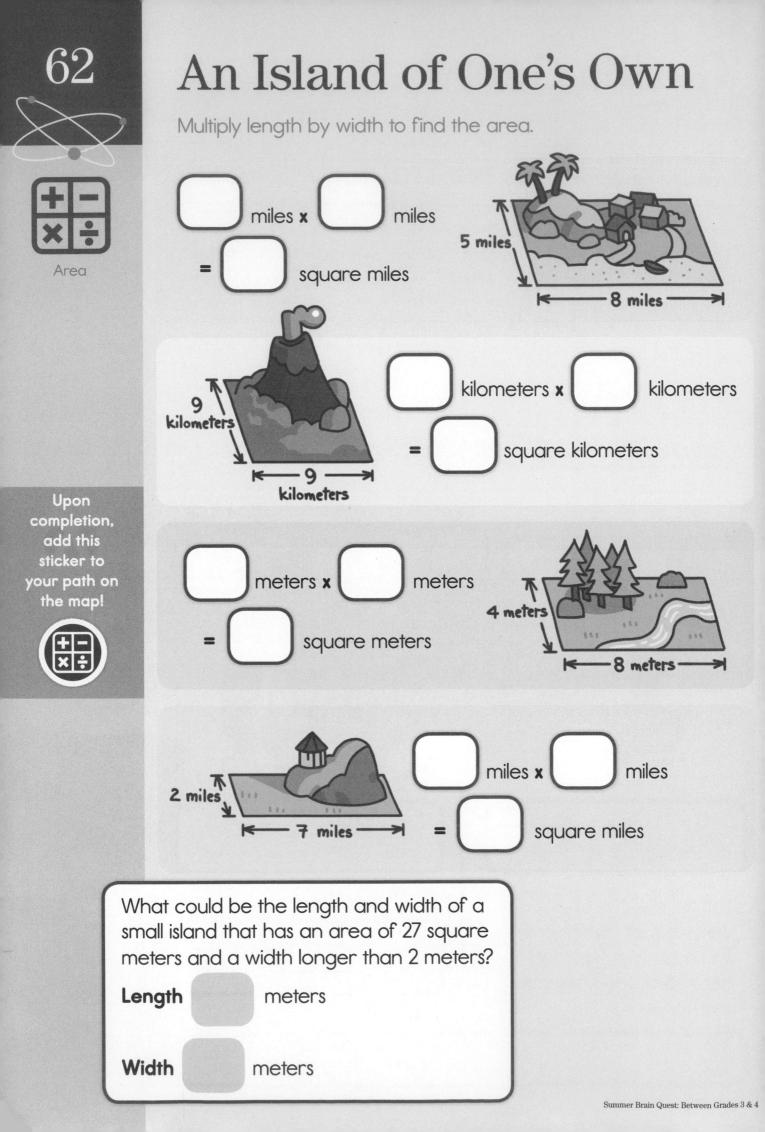

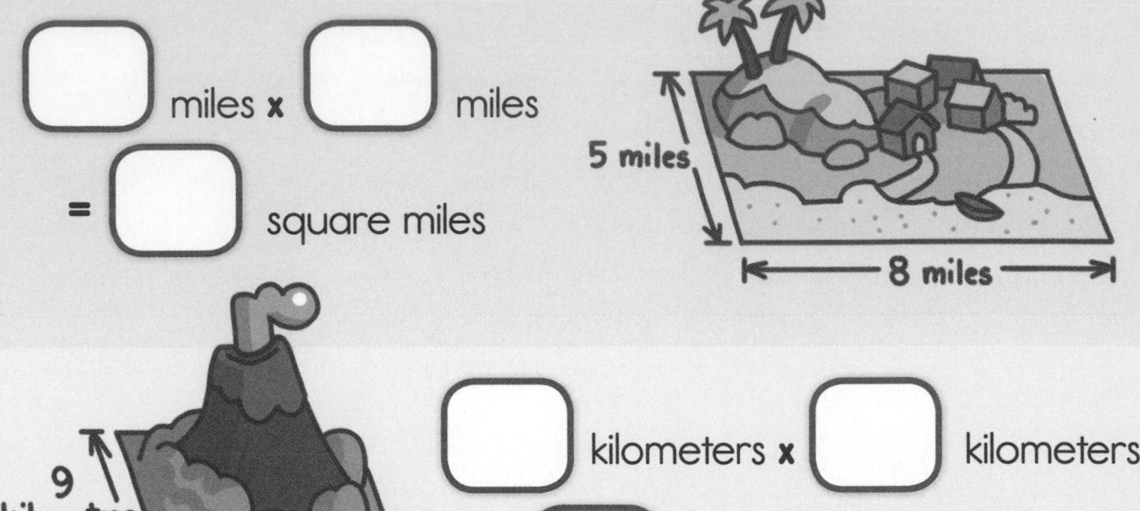

☐ miles x ☐ miles
= ☐ square miles

9 kilometers
9 kilometers

☐ kilometers x ☐ kilometers
= ☐ square kilometers

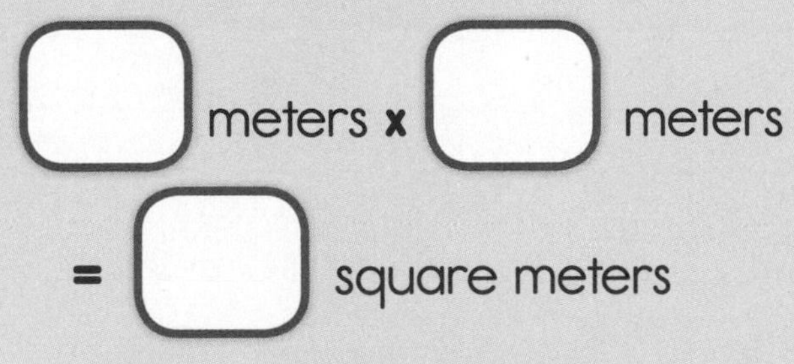

☐ meters x ☐ meters
= ☐ square meters

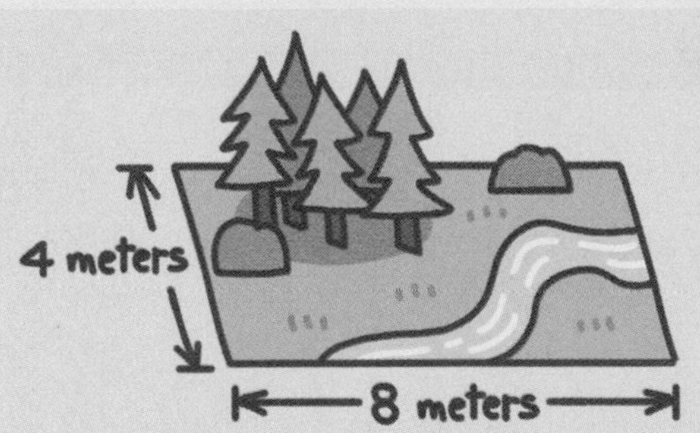

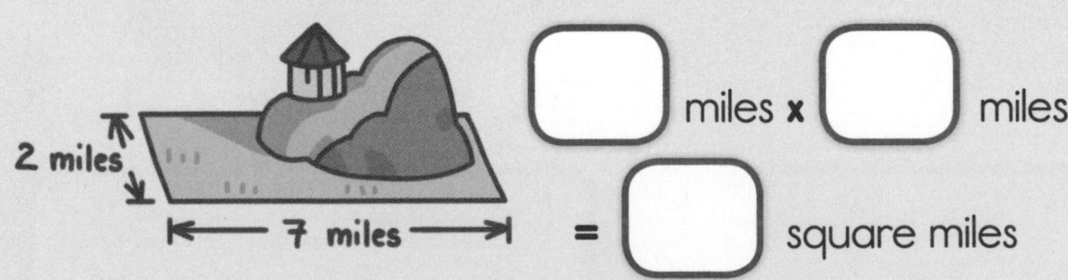

☐ miles x ☐ miles
= ☐ square miles

Upon completion, add this sticker to your path on the map!

What could be the length and width of a small island that has an area of 27 square meters and a width longer than 2 meters?

Length ☐ meters

Width ☐ meters

For Real?

Draw a line to match each figurative statement with its literal meaning.

Literal and Figurative Language

The cook is a miracle worker.	We've been at sea for a long time.
We've been sailing out here forever.	I always wanted to be a sailor.
If they put me on night watch again, I'm going to die of boredom.	I think the captain is mean.
The captain is a monster.	I get bored on night watch.
I was born a sailor.	The cook is talented.

Upon completion, add this sticker to your path on the map!

Brain Box

Literal language uses words to communicate an exact and factual meaning. **Figurative language** uses symbolic words or exaggerations to express a new or different meaning.

Happy New Year!

Use proofreading marks to capitalize letters and add the missing commas, periods, apostrophes, and quotation marks.

Punctuation and Capitalization

Symbol	a (triple underline)	^ ,	⊙	' V	“ ” V V
What it means	capitalize	Add a comma	Add a period	Add an apostrophe	Add quotation marks

lunar new year celebrations happen every year starting on the night before the year ends

family members will clean each familys house to sweep away bad fortune

people greet each other by saying things like peace all year round

on the first day of the celebration fireworks are set off to chase away bad spirits

the holiday is celebrated in many asian countries and asian communities all around the world

the lunar new years last celebration is the lantern festival

to celebrate people light lanterns of all kinds including some that float away on lakes or streams

Upon completion, add this sticker to your path on the map!

Festival of Lights

Spelling

Circle the correctly spelled word to complete each sentence.

Hindus around the world enjoy Diwali **evry** **every** year.

The festival **celebraits** **celebrates** the victory of light over darkness.

Families put on their best **clothes** **cloths** .

Than **Then** they gather with their community for a feast.

Around the world, people light lamps and candles on the **roofs** **rooves** of their houses, outside their doors, and around temples.

The shining of light in the dark symbolizes the triumph of **knowlege** **knowledge** over ignorance and hope over despair.

Upon completion, add this sticker to your path on the map!

BONUS: Circle each correctly spelled word.

Ancient Greeks didn't worship **their** **they're** god Pan in the **citys** **cities**—only in the countryside, **becuase** **becuse** **because** he was the god of the wild.

Now add this sticker to your map!

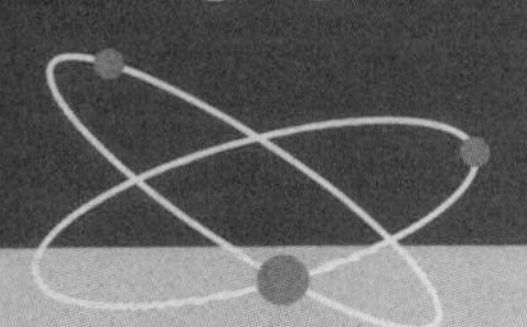

Serpent Trails

Write an equation to find the perimeter of each shape. Then calculate the perimeter.

Perimeter

Upon completion, add this sticker to your path on the map!

P = ______ = ______ feet

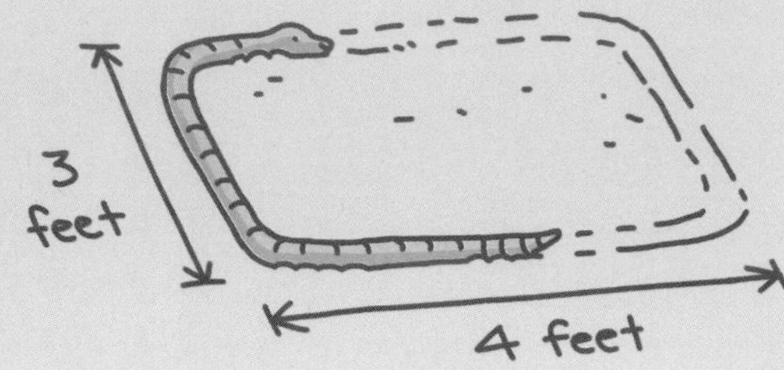

P = ______ = ______ feet

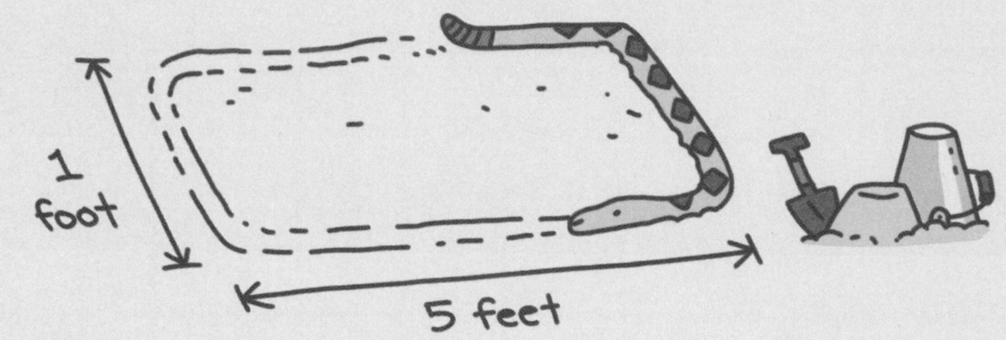

P = ______ = ______ feet

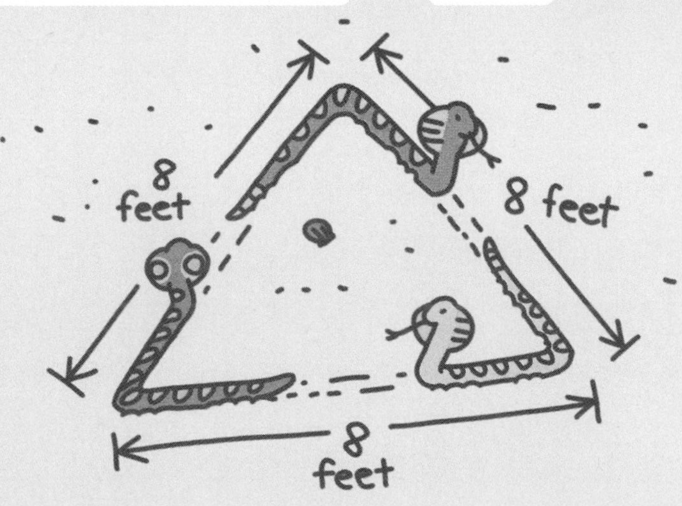

A rectangle has long sides that are 5 feet long. Its perimeter is 14 feet. What is the length of its short sides?

______ feet

Brain Box

The **perimeter** is the distance around a figure. You can use any of these equations to find the perimeter of a rectangle, where ***P* = perimeter**, ***l* = length**, and ***w* = width**:

$$P = l + w + l + w$$

or

$$P = 2l + 2w$$

or

$$P = 2(l + w)$$

Level 4A complete!

Add this achievement sticker to your path…

…and move on to

Level 5A

on page 78!

. . . OR GO ON AN OUTSIDE QUEST AND MOVE ON TO LEVEL 5B ON PAGE 92!

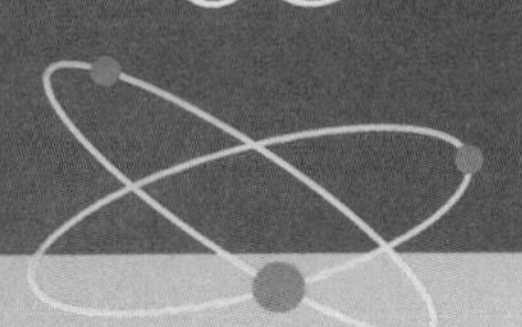

Unit Fractions

Sea Turtles

Draw a line to match each shaded part of a shape with a fraction.

START LEVEL 4B HERE!

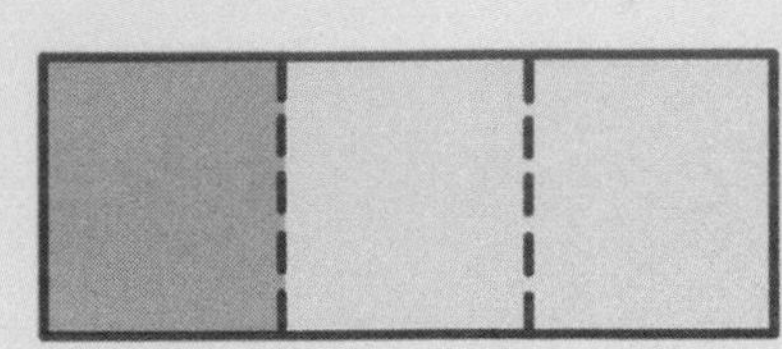

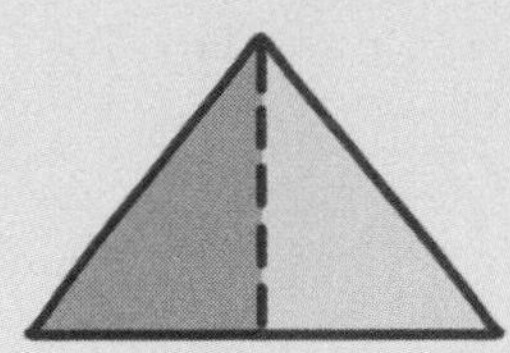

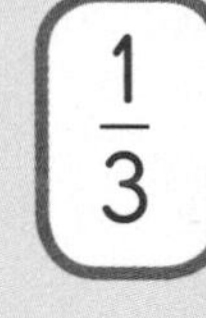

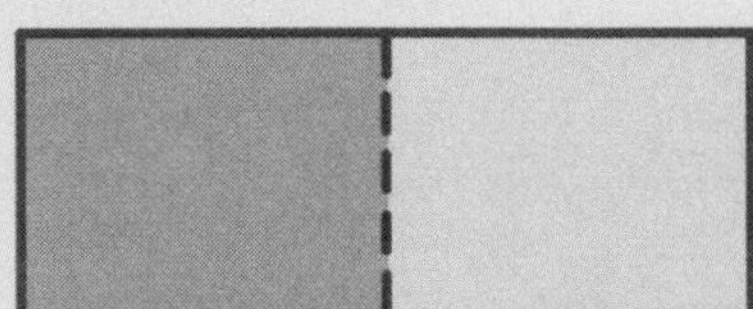

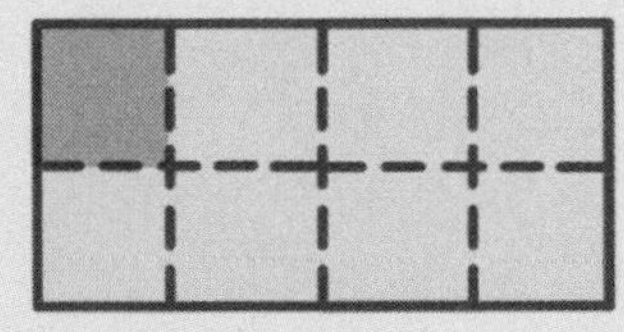

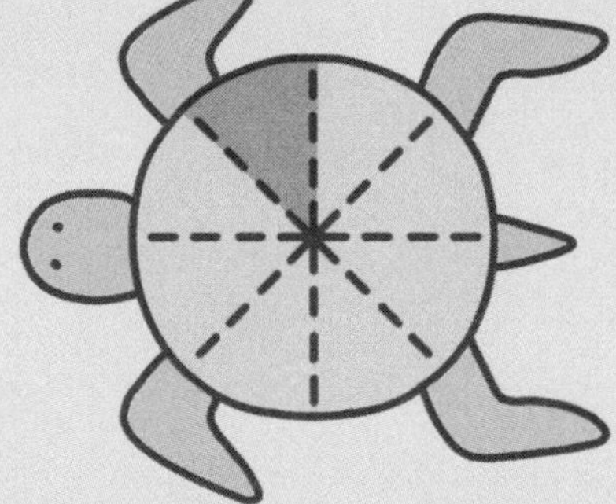

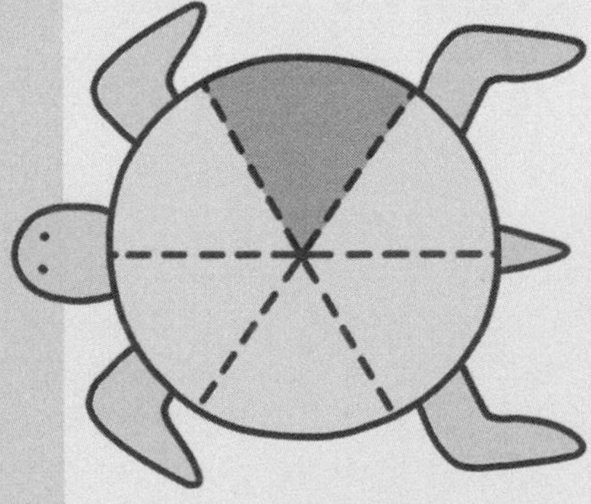

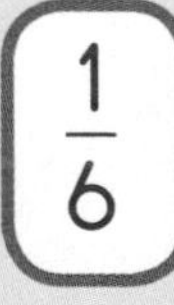

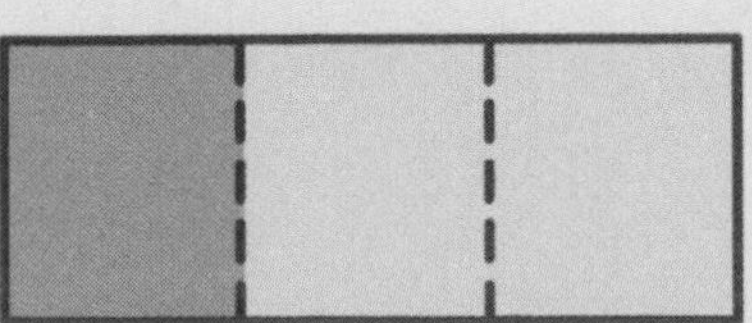

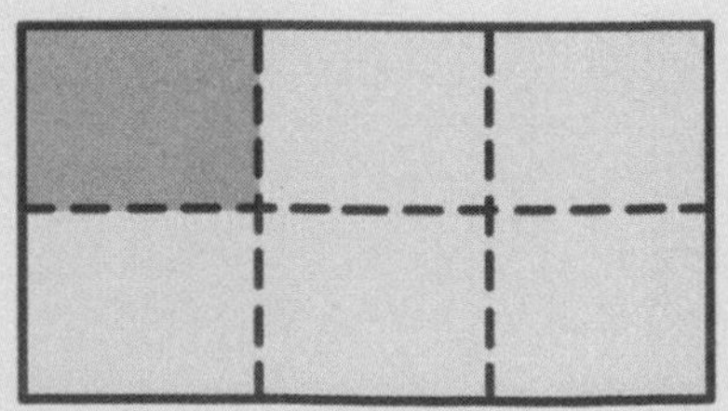

Design the Tags

Color each shape to show the fraction.

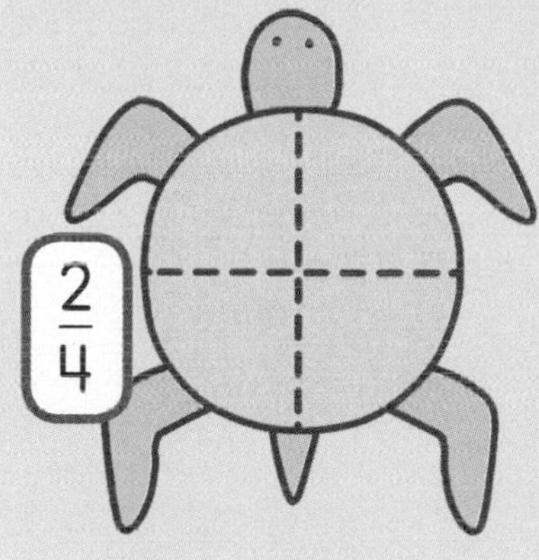

Fractions

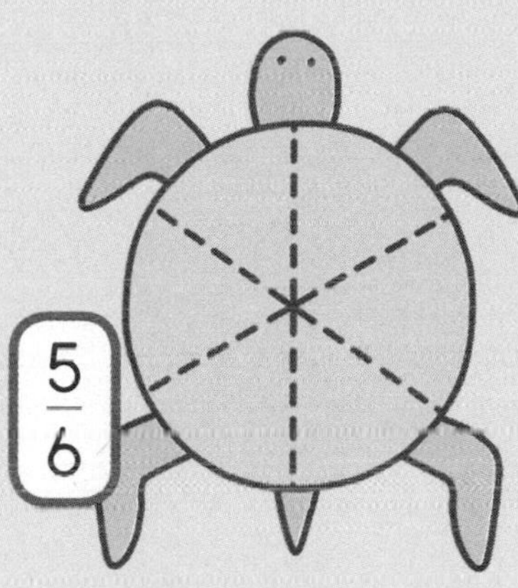

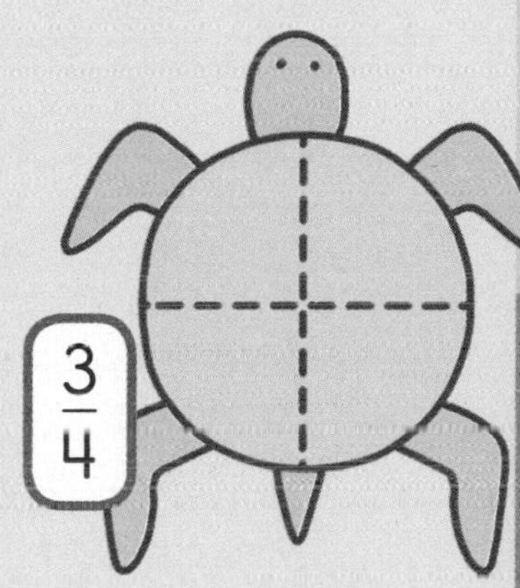

Upon completion, add these stickers to your path on the map!

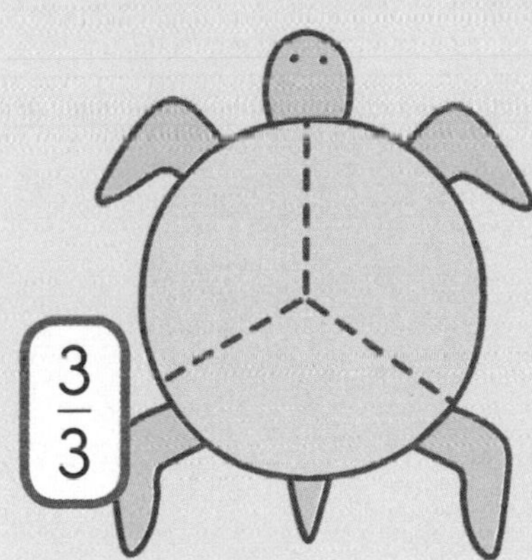

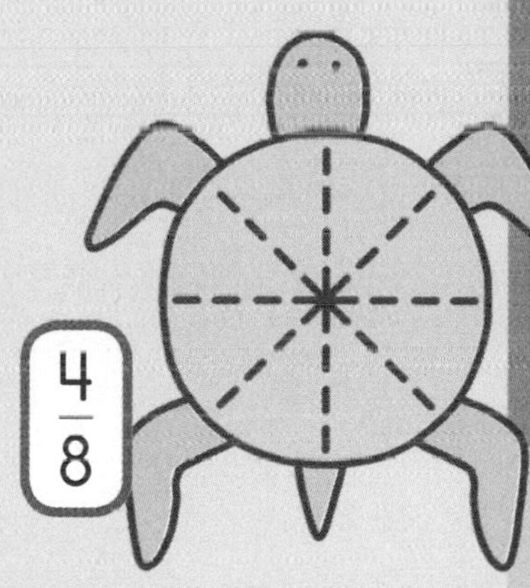

Color parts of the shape in red, blue, and yellow.
Then write the fraction of the shape that each color covers.

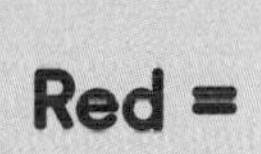

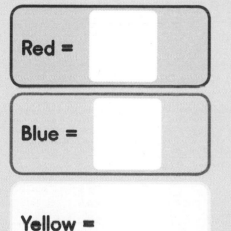

Red =

Blue =

Yellow =

70

Better Than One

Read the passage. Then complete the sentences.

Animal Groups and Survival

Primates are a group of animals that have large brains relative to other animals. They depend on their sense of sight more than their sense of smell. Many of them also have opposable thumbs (thumbs that grow opposite the other fingers of the hand and make it easy to grasp things).

Most primates also live together in tight-knit social groups. These groups give members many advantages for survival, such as allowing primates to hunt together, share knowledge and solve conflicts, help each other care for their young and old, protect against predators, and keep each other company.

If two gorillas have a conflict with each other, the leader gorilla can ____________________________.

If an enemy threatens, several gorillas together can ____________________________.

If a gorilla infant loses a parent, the other parent or other gorillas can ____________________________.

When looking for food, several gorillas can ____________________________.

By ________________________, an infant gorilla can learn more from the group than from just his or her parents.

Upon completion, add this sticker to your path on the map!

BONUS: Unlike gorillas, most squid do not live in groups. But they have to come together at least once in order for their species to survive. Do they need to come together to gather food, to be social, or to reproduce?

____

Now add this sticker to your map!

Ghost Boats in the Desert

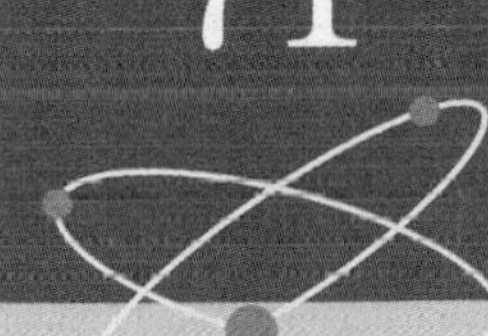

Read the story. Then write the missing dates on the timeline.

Sequencing Events

Would you ever expect to find a fleet of Egyptian boats buried in the desert? Well, in 2000 CE, archaeologists discovered 14 of them! The boats had been buried, probably around 2500 BCE, as part of the funeral ceremony for a pharaoh. The boats were placed with their noses facing the Nile, so that the pharaoh could join the sun god Ra and sail down the Nile into the afterlife. How did the archaeologists find the boats after all those years? Well, they had some help! In 1988 CE, wind began to blow sand away from the mud brick walls that surrounded the boats—giving archaeologists a clue to where to look!

Upon completion, add this sticker to your path on the map!

BONUS: Circle which came first:

Around 1300 BCE, Mesopotamians used the earliest known sailboats to fish in deep waters.

Around 4000 BCE, Egyptians came up with the idea of attaching a sail to a simple boat.

Now add this sticker to your map!

Brain Box

BCE is the abbreviation for Before the Common Era (or before the year 1 on the common Western calendar—there was no year zero). **CE** is the abbreviation for Common Era (or the year 1 and after on the common Western calendar). For example, 1000 BCE is further in the past than 500 BCE.

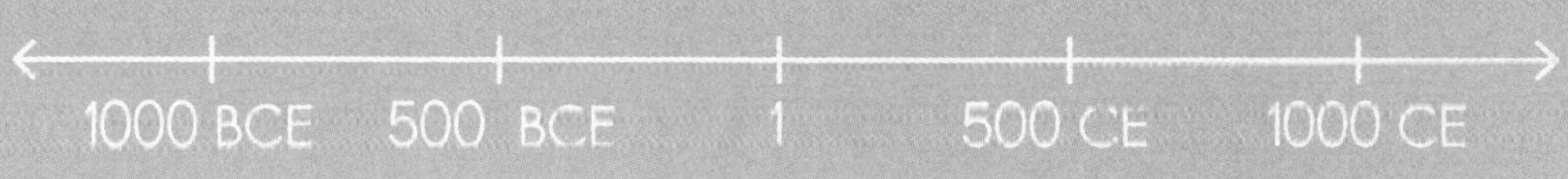

1000 BCE | 500 BCE | 1 | 500 CE | 1000 CE

Night of Knights

Fill in each highlighted word to complete each sentence.

Homophones

It's __________ __________ outside the castle walls! **quiet** **quite**

__________ we almost to __________ dragon's lair? **our** **are**

__________ they said they were more worried about getting past the dragon __________ they were about finding their way home.

than **then**

The __________ dragons are running __________ the castle, __________! **to** **too** **two**

The ______________ monk ______________ when the dragon breathed fire at him. **bald** **bawled**

Upon completion, add this sticker to your path on the map!

Brain Box

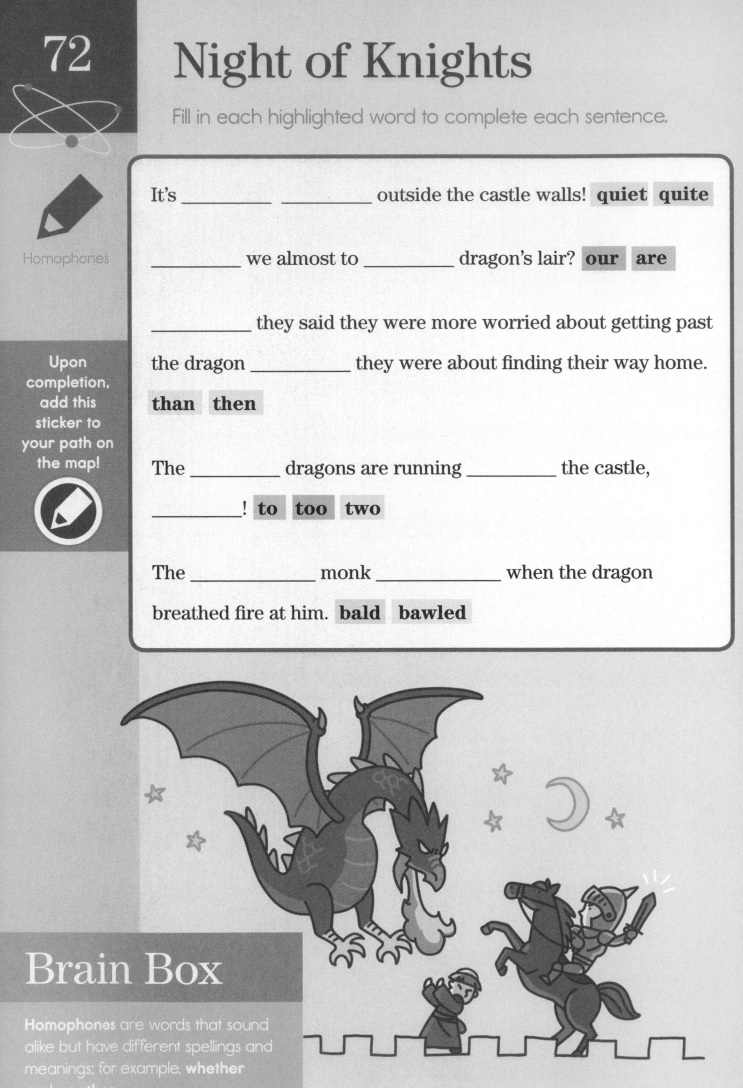

Homophones are words that sound alike but have different spellings and meanings; for example, **whether** and **weather**.

Fractions Ahoy!

Label each number line with fractions. Then follow the directions to draw an object in the correct location.

Number Line Fractions

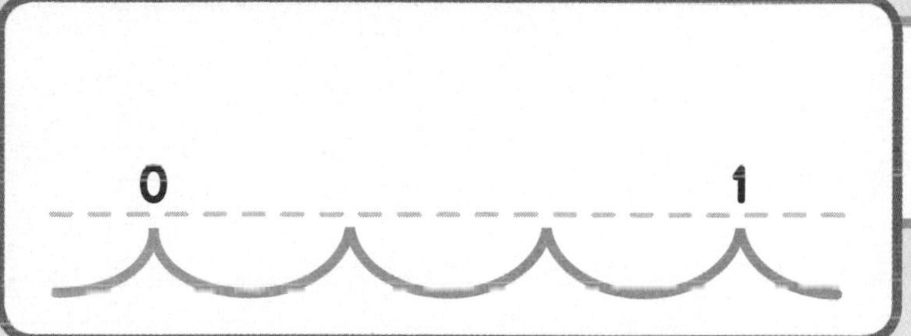

Draw a sailing ship at the $\frac{2}{3}$ point.

Draw a seabird at the $\frac{3}{4}$ point.

Upon completion, add this sticker to your path on the map!

Draw a jumping fish at the $\frac{3}{6}$ point.

0 1

BONUS: Label the number line. Then draw Poseidon's trident at the $\frac{5}{8}$ point.

0 1

Now add this sticker to your map!

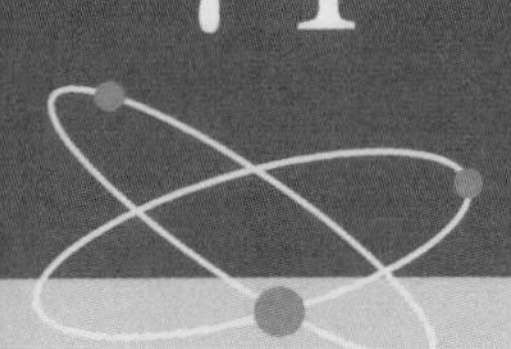

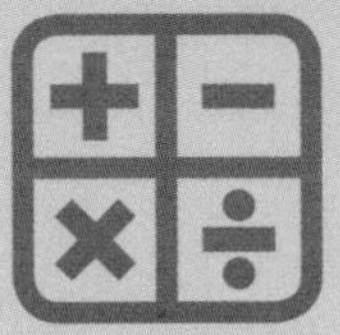

Comparing Fractions

Ancient Fractions

Write a fraction to show how much of each tablet is filled with hieroglyphics. Then write <, =, or > to show the relationship between the fractions.

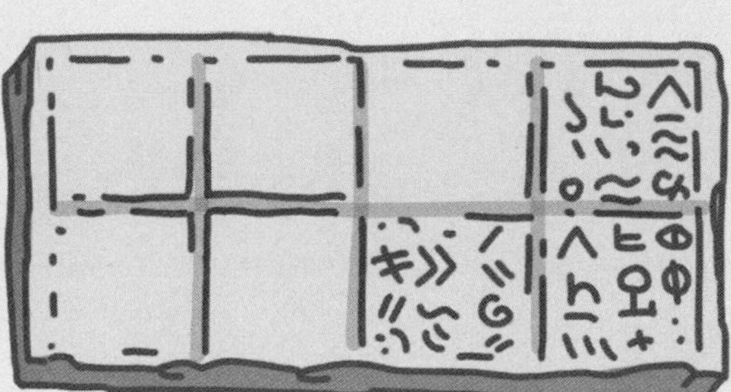

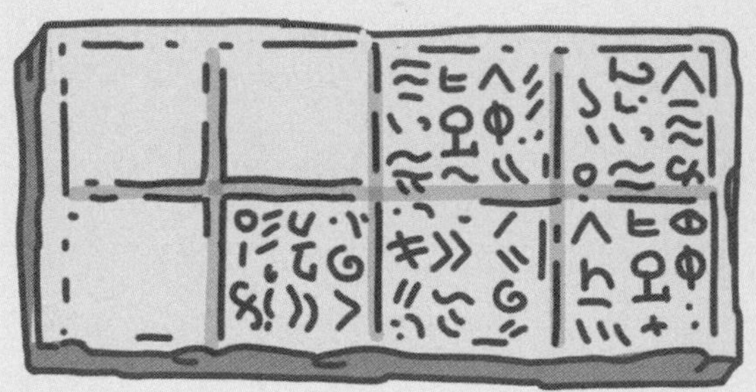

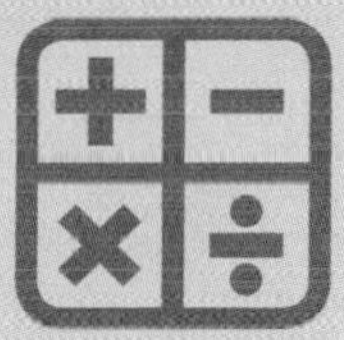

Comparing Fractions

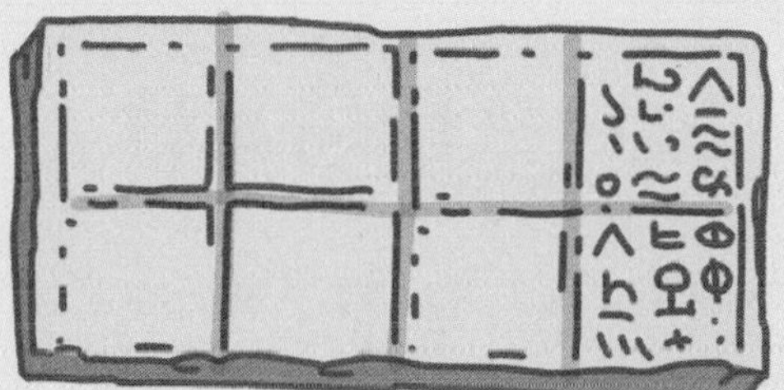
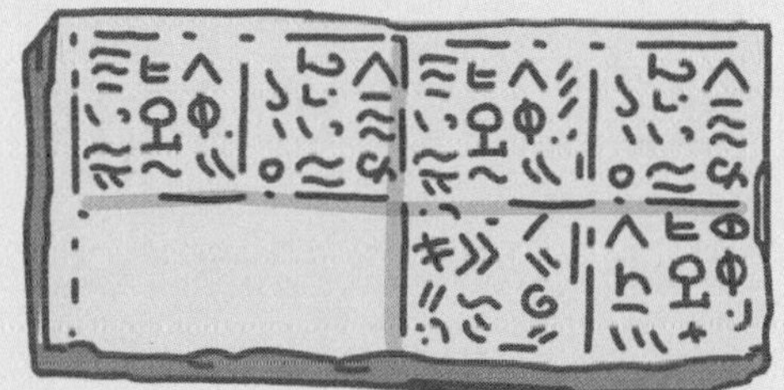

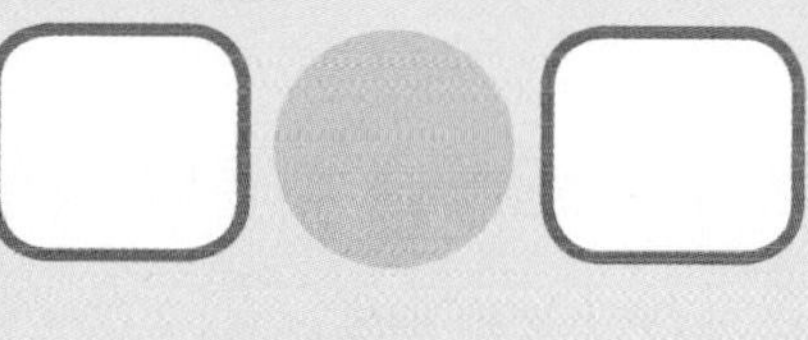

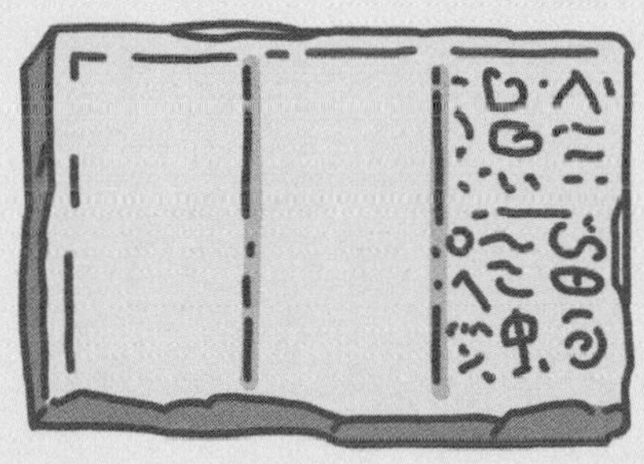

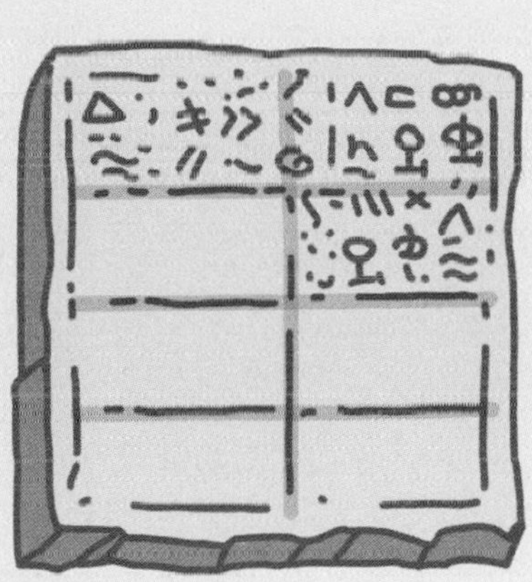

Upon completion, add these stickers to your path on the map!

Brain Box

The symbol < means less than.

The symbol > means greater than.

The symbol = means equal to.

Learning the Language

Read each sentence. Then use context clues to define each bold nautical word or phrase and write the matching definition from the box.

Context Clues

tool that measures latitude	damage	sailor
ship that gets ahead of others	change direction	

We're going the wrong direction. We need to come about.

"Come about" ______________________________

Upon completion, add this sticker to your path on the map!

This sail is a mess. Look at all the chafing.

"Chafing" ______________________________

He's been working on boats all his life. He's a real mariner.

"Mariner" ______________________________

Look how far ahead that ship has sailed from the rest. What a romper.

"Romper" ______________________________

I need to calculate our latitude. Hand me the sextant.

"Sextant" ______________________________

Brain Box

Sometimes you can figure out what a word or phrase means by looking at the surrounding words, or **context clues**. Often the words directly before and after an unknown word give enough information to explain the word's meaning.

Level 4B complete!

Add this achievement sticker to your path…

. . . AND GO ON AN OUTSIDE QUEST AND MOVE ON TO LEVEL 5A ON PAGE 78!

…or move on to

Level 5B

on page 92!

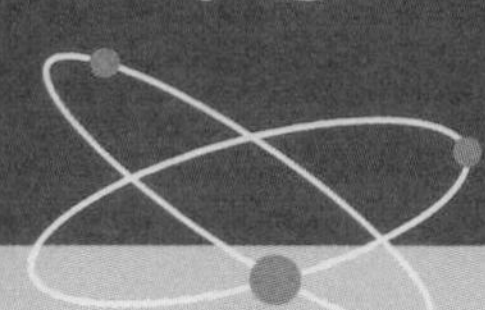

Storied Spider

Read the excerpts featuring Anansi, the spider from Ghanaian folktales. Then write whether the excerpt is a poem, drama, or prose.

Poems, Drama, and Prose

START LEVEL 5A HERE!

Upon completion, add this sticker to your path on the map!

Anansi is the most clever
creature of all time.
Wherever, whomever, whenever,
he'll outsmart you every time!

____

There once was a time when there were no stories on Earth. The sky god, Nyame, had kept them all for himself. One day, Anansi the spider asked Nyame for his stories, so he could share them with the world. But Nyame said his stories cost a fortune—much too much money for a spider! Nevertheless, Anansi asked him how much they cost, and . . .

____

ANANSI (looking into Rabbit's pot): Those greens look delicious!

RABBIT: They're not quite done. But if you come back later, I can give you some.

____

Brain Box

Poetry is a form of writing that has rhythm and sometimes rhymes. **Prose** does not have rhythm and is usually presented in sentences and paragraphs. **Drama** can be written as a script for a performance.

BONUS: If a folktale about a flying carpet was told all in rhyme, would it be prose or poetry?

____

Now add this sticker to your map!

Be Resourceful!

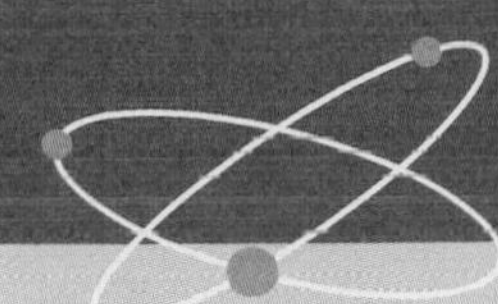

Look at each picture. Then write whether it features natural, human, or capital resources.

If you could have only one of the resources shown above to start a civilization with, which would you choose, and why?

Natural, Human, and Capital Resources

Upon completion, add this sticker to your path on the map!

Brain Box

Natural resources come from the earth. **Human resources** are what people have to offer, such as labor or talent. **Capital resources** are money and goods that can be traded.

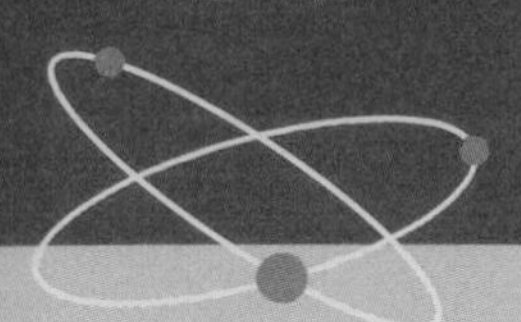

Measurement

Math Oasis

Write the number of liters of water in each jug. Then write an equation to solve each question.

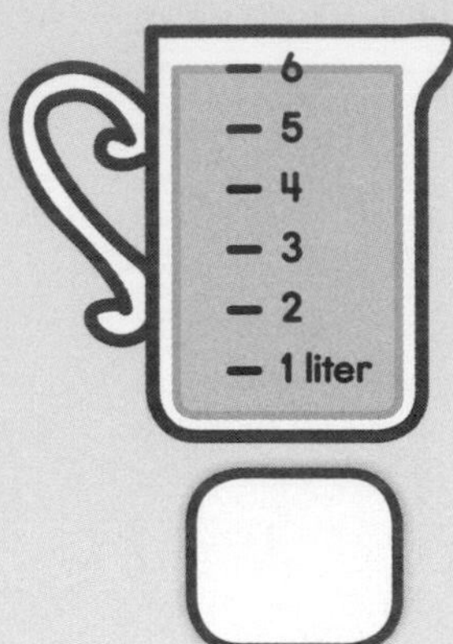

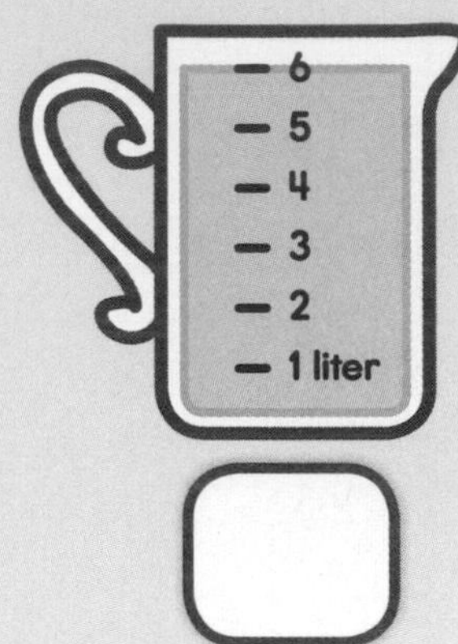

How much water is there in all?

___ + ___ = ___ liters

How much water will each explorer get if 3 explorers share the total?

___ ÷ ___ = ___ liters

Upon completion, add this sticker to your path on the map!

How much water is there in all?

___ + ___ + ___ = ___ liters

How much water will each explorer get if 5 explorers share the total?

___ ÷ ___ = ___ liters

Brain Box

Customary measures of **liquid volume** are ounces, cups, pints, quarts, and gallons. A metric measure of liquid volume is liters.

Changing the World

Read the passage. Then look at each picture and write a possible result of the human impact on the landscape.

Human beings, while small, have a history of making enormous changes to the geography (the physical features) of the planet. For centuries, mankind has built large structures, including pyramids and dams. The scale of these projects has changed entire landscapes. People have dug giant holes in the earth to facilitate mining for minerals and fuels. People have blasted pathways through mountain ranges to build railroads and expressways. Some changes are not on purpose—humans throughout history have created mountains of waste from these ventures and other activities, too.

Human Impact

Upon completion, add this sticker to your path on the map!

BONUS: If the pharaoh ordered that the broken rubble from a construction site be used to repave roads in Egypt, would it cut down on waste or change a natural feature of the landscape?

Now add this sticker to your map!

Pyramid Shapes

Shapes: Categories

Sort each gem by its shape. Write its name in the correct hidden chamber. A gem can be sorted in more than one chamber.

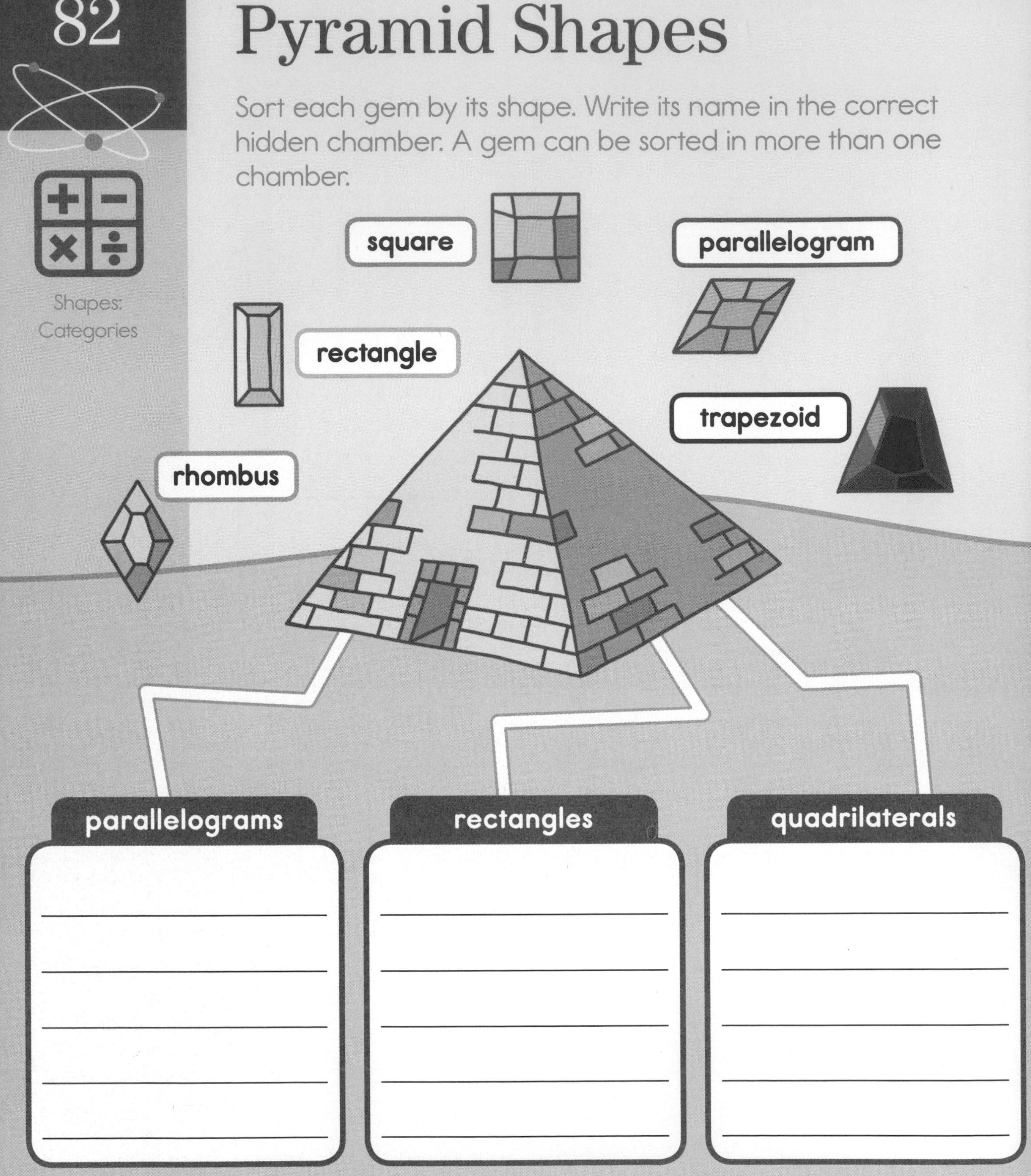

Brain Box

A **quadrilateral** is any flat, closed, four-sided figure with straight sides. A **parallelogram** is a quadrilateral with opposite sides that are parallel and equal in length. A **rectangle** is a parallelogram with only right angles (square corners). A **rhombus** is a parallelogram with equal sides. A **square** is a rectangle with equal sides.

Draw each quadrilateral according to the description.

A quadrilateral with only one square corner

A quadrilateral with all square corners

A quadrilateral with only one pair of parallel sides

A quadrilateral with one pair of parallel sides and two square corners

Shapes: Attributes

Upon completion, add these stickers to your path on the map!

BONUS: To build a pyramid, Egyptians carved rectangular blocks out of irregularly shaped stone. Draw an irregular quadrilateral that has no parallel sides and no sides with equal lengths. Then draw a rectangle inside it.

Now add this sticker to your map!

84

What Do You Want to Know?

Research

Read the passage and examples. Then write a research question for each of the topics.

Research is a process of gaining knowledge by searching for and gathering new information. Being a researcher is like being a detective who is investigating a little-known or little-understood topic. But no matter the topic, research always begins with the same thing: a good question. A good question for research cannot be answered with a simple yes or no—you will need to look for answers in a few sources. You might need to read newspapers, look up facts and figures on the Internet, visit a new place, or talk to people to hear their perspective or point of view. When you're on the hunt for more information, finding the answer often inspires a new question!

BONUS: Choose one of the topics and questions on the next page. Then write three things you might do to find the answer to your question.

Research

Topic: Ancient Egyptian government

Question: Who was the most powerful person in the ancient Egyptian government?

Topic: Ancient Egyptian buildings

Question: How were ancient Egyptian buildings designed and built?

Topic: Ancient Egyptian schools

Question: ______________________________

____

Topic: Ancient Egyptian children

Question: ______________________________

____

Topic: Ancient Egyptian sports

Question: ______________________________

____

Topic: Ancient Egyptian pets

Question: ______________________________

____

Upon completion, add these stickers to your path on the map!

____

____

____

Now add this sticker to your map!

Eyes to See

Read each explorer's letter. Then answer each question.

Comparing Two Accounts

Dear National Geosophic Society,

Thank you so much for your support of our expedition. After traveling across the trackless desert, we reached the palace, which was covered with strange carvings and sparkled in the sunset. The next morning, we moved quickly through the chambers until we found the royal library. It was just where my research predicted: in a large vault under the royal throne room. Amazingly, the place had never been found by other explorers. All the shelves were still full of poetry, maps, and books on botany in dozens of languages. We even found a half-finished page that a scribe must have left behind. It will take years for us to read through the books, but who knows what treasures we'll find within!

Sincerely,

Sara

Dear Explorer's Association,

I'm writing to give you the results of your investment in our expedition.

We knew at once that we had reached the palace when we saw the stone sparkling in the sunset. My research told of treasure chambers containing untold riches, including the precious turquoise mask of the queen. But after searching for days, we found nothing more than a few small boxes of coins and jewelry. The place had been thoroughly looted, with nothing left but the books on the bookshelves and designs that had been painted or carved on the walls. We left very disappointed, with barely enough to cover the expenses of our expedition.

Sincerely,

John

What do both accounts mention about the palace?

____

____

What details does Sara mention about her first sighting of the palace that John does not?

____

____

What does John most want to find in the palace?

____

____

What does John find in the palace instead?

____

____

What does Sara think is the biggest treasure in the palace?

____

____

Comparing Two Accounts

Upon completion, add these stickers to your path on the map!

BONUS: Imagine that Sara and John go on to discover a hidden chamber, which is full of treasure and strange scrolls about griffins and other legendary creatures. Based on their accounts on the previous page, make a prediction—what do you think each explorer would be most interested in? Explain why.

____

____

____

____

Data: Scaled Picture Graphs

The Pharaoh's Pets

The picture graph below shows the number of royal pets the pharaoh owns. Use the graph to answer each question.

NUMBER OF ROYAL PETS

Cat	🐾 🐾 🐾 🐾 🐾 🐾 🐾 🐾
Dog	🐾 🐾
Monkey	🐾 🐾 🐾

Each 🐾 stands for 2 pets.

How many royal dogs are there? ________

Which royal pet is most likely the favorite type of pet? ________

How many royal pets altogether does the graph represent? ________

How many fewer dogs than monkeys are owned by the pharaoh? ________

If there were 2 more royal monkeys, how many paw prints altogether would there be next to the monkey? ________

Can You Dig It?

Draw bars on the graph to show the number of each dug-up artifact. Then answer each question.

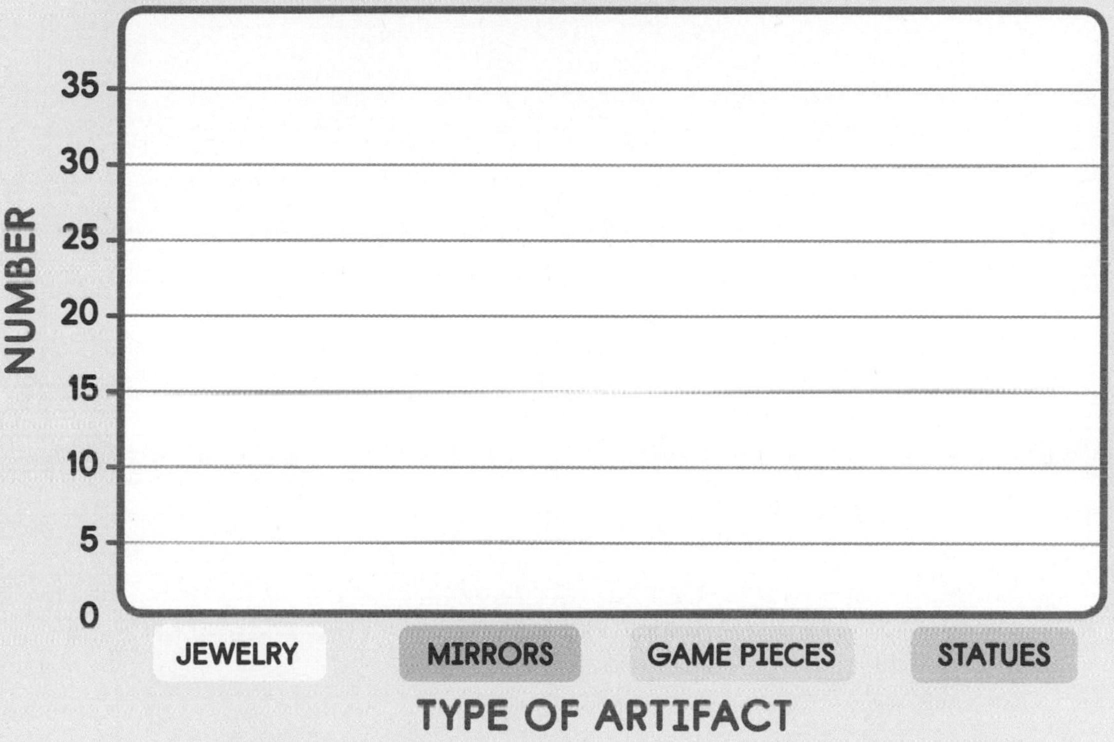

Data: Scaled Bar Graphs

Jewelry	Game pieces	Mirrors	Statues
25	30	10	15

NUMBER: 0, 5, 10, 15, 20, 25, 30, 35

JEWELRY | MIRRORS | GAME PIECES | STATUES

TYPE OF ARTIFACT

Upon completion, add these stickers to your path on the map!

If the archaeologists had found 13 fewer game pieces, how many game pieces would they have? _______

If the archaeologists found 2 more mirrors and 3 more pieces of jewelry, how many mirrors and pieces of jewelry would they have in all? _______

If the archaeologists had 17 instead of 15 small statues, between which two lines would the top of the bar appear on the graph?

____

How to Make Pancakes . . . in Ancient Greece

Read the ancient Greek recipe. Then answer each question.

Informational Reading

Ingredients

1 cup flour

1 cup water

2 tablespoons honey

5–6 tablespoons olive oil

Directions

Make a batter by mixing the flour, water, and 1 tablespoon of honey. Pour oil into a pan and heat it. When it is hot, pour a small amount of the batter into the pan. Allow it to thicken as it cooks. When it thickens, flip it. Continue to turn the pancake until it is golden brown on both sides. Remove the pancake from the pan. Repeat with the rest of the batter. Drizzle the remaining honey over the finished pancakes and serve piping hot!

Which ingredient is used first, oil or flour?

____

Which ingredient is not part of the batter?

____

How do you know when your pancakes are done?

____

Would your pancakes still turn out well if you took out two sentences in the middle of the recipe? Why or why not?

____

____

Would your pancakes still turn out well if you took the first three sentences and put them at the end, instead of the beginning? Why or why not?

____

____

Upon completion, add this sticker to your path on the map!

Level 5A complete!

Add this achievement sticker to your path…

…and move on to

Level 6

on page 106!

Your Unlimited Potential

Read the passage. Then write **K** next to the objects that have **kinetic energy**, and write **P** next to the objects that have **potential energy**.

Potential Energy

When a boulder is still atop a hill, it doesn't look very energetic, but it's filled with energy—**potential energy**. Potential energy is energy that can be put into motion. Unlike **kinetic energy** (the energy of motion), potential energy is stored and simply waiting to happen. A boulder that is at the top of a hill has gravitational energy stored in it—at any moment it could roll and plunge down the hill. As soon as the boulder begins to move, the potential energy has converted to kinetic energy. Lots of objects have potential energy stored in them—gasoline and food have chemical energy waiting to be released, and stretched rubber bands and coils store mechanical energy.

START LEVEL 5B HERE!

Upon completion, add this sticker to your path on the map!

Name three examples of potential energy around you now.

____

____

____

Name three examples of kinetic energy around you now.

____

____

____

Arctic Time

Write the time shown on the clock for these activities in an Inuit community. Include a.m. and p.m.

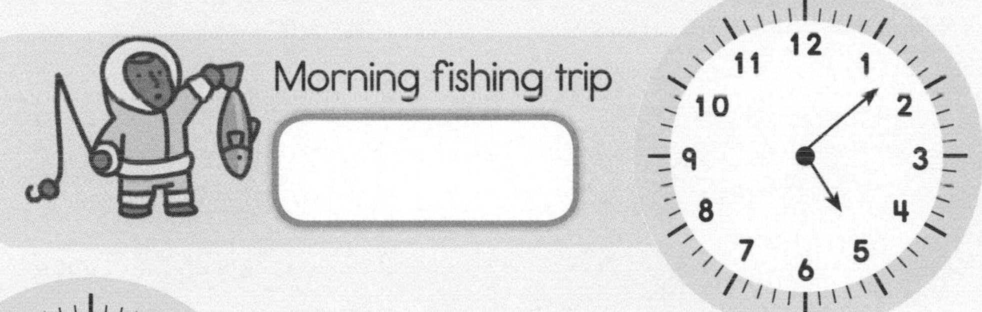

Morning fishing trip

Time

Morning language lesson

Lunch

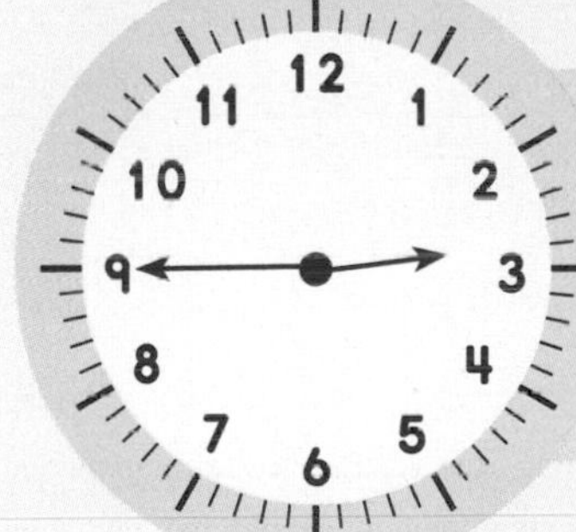

Playing games after school

Upon completion, add this sticker to your path on the map!

Evening square dancing

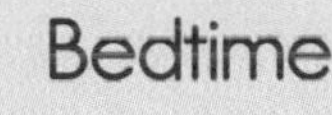

Bedtime

Brain Box

The hours between 12:00 midnight and 12:00 noon are **a.m.** hours.

The hours between 12:00 noon and 12:00 midnight are **p.m.** hours.

Timeless Art

Answer each word problem.

Time

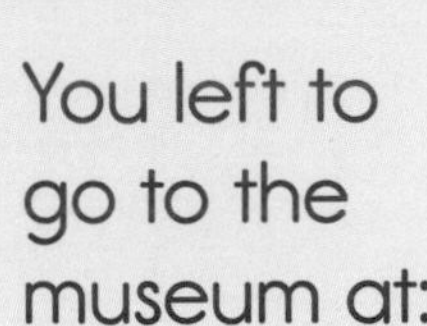

Your watch says:

The Inuit Art Museum opens this morning in 40 minutes. What time will the museum open?

You left to go to the museum at:

It takes a half hour to get there. What time will you arrive?

You attended a painting workshop. It began at 10:04 a.m. and ended at 10:33 a.m. How long was the workshop? ___ minutes

Upon completion, add this sticker to your path on the map!

You stopped for lunch at 11:45 a.m. You left the museum café at 12:39 p.m. How many minutes did you spend at lunch? ___ minutes

BONUS: Use the number line below to answer the question.

You spent 22 minutes less than an hour viewing a film about ancient stone sculptures called *inuksuk*. If the film started at 1:00 p.m., what time did it end?

Now add this sticker to your map!

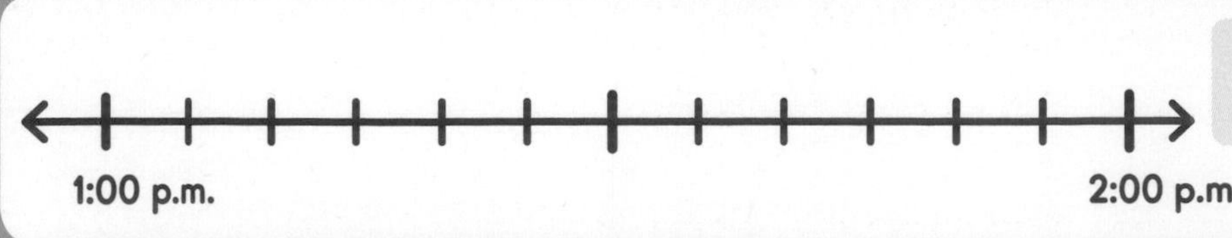

The Land of Nod

Read the poem by Robert Louis Stevenson. Then answer each question.

Stanzas

From breakfast on through all the day
At home among my friends I stay,
But every night I go abroad
Afar into the land of Nod.

All by myself I have to go,
With none to tell me what to do—
All alone beside the streams
And up the mountain-sides of dreams.

The strangest things are there for me
Both things to eat and things to see,
And many frightening sights abroad
Till morning in the land of Nod.

Try as I like to find the way,
I never can get back by day,
Nor can remember plain and clear
The curious music that I hear.

Upon completion, add this sticker to your path on the map!

What is the land of Nod? Which stanza or stanzas show evidence of your answer? ______________________________

____

____

From reading the first stanza only, where might you think the land of Nod is? ______________________________

What does the poet find in the land of Nod?

____

____

What does the poet say about returning to the land of Nod? ______________________________

____

____

Brain Box

A **poem** sometimes uses **rhyming**, **rhythm**, and **alliteration** to tie things together. A **stanza** is a group of lines in a poem.

A Changing Map

Read the passage and study the map of the approximate locations of some of the major tribes prior to contact with European colonists. Then answer each question.

Native American History and Culture

We're used to looking at a map of the United States that includes names of states like Maine, Alabama, and Oregon. But before Europeans arrived on the continent, different groups of Native Americans lived in their own cities and communities from the Atlantic to the Pacific. Many of the names on our present-day map are derived from the indigenous languages of these Native American tribes.

Groups in a specific region may have had cultural similarities, like the Lakota, Cheyenne, and Comanche, who all lived in the Great Plains and followed buffalo herds. However, there was lots of diversity among the tribes of the North American continent, including different languages, cultural practices, and lifestyles. For example, there were nomadic groups in the Great Plains, while most tribes lived in one place and farmed domesticated crops.

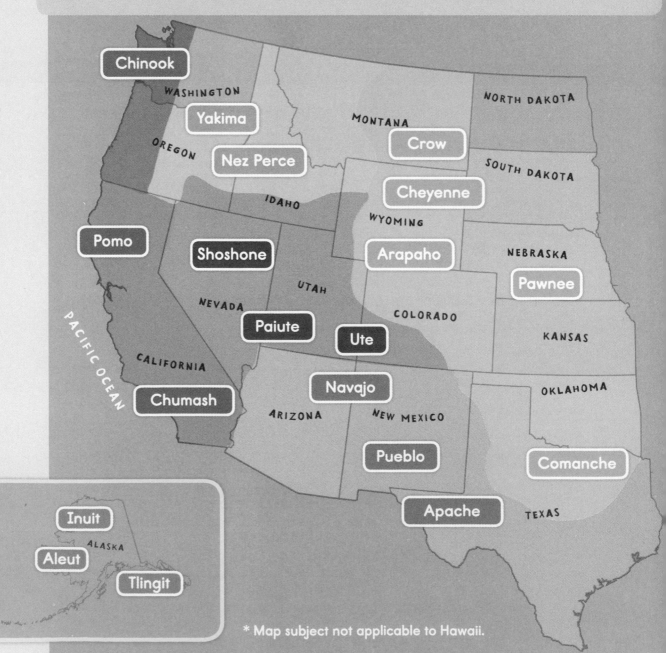

Native American History and Culture

Which tribes lived in what is now Texas?

____

What tribal name now forms the name of an East Coast state?

____

Did the Miami tribe live in the same state as the modern city of Miami? If not, which tribe lived on the current site of the city of Miami?

____

Which people lived in states that included Georgia, Tennessee, North Carolina, and South Carolina?

____

Upon completion, add these stickers to your path on the map!

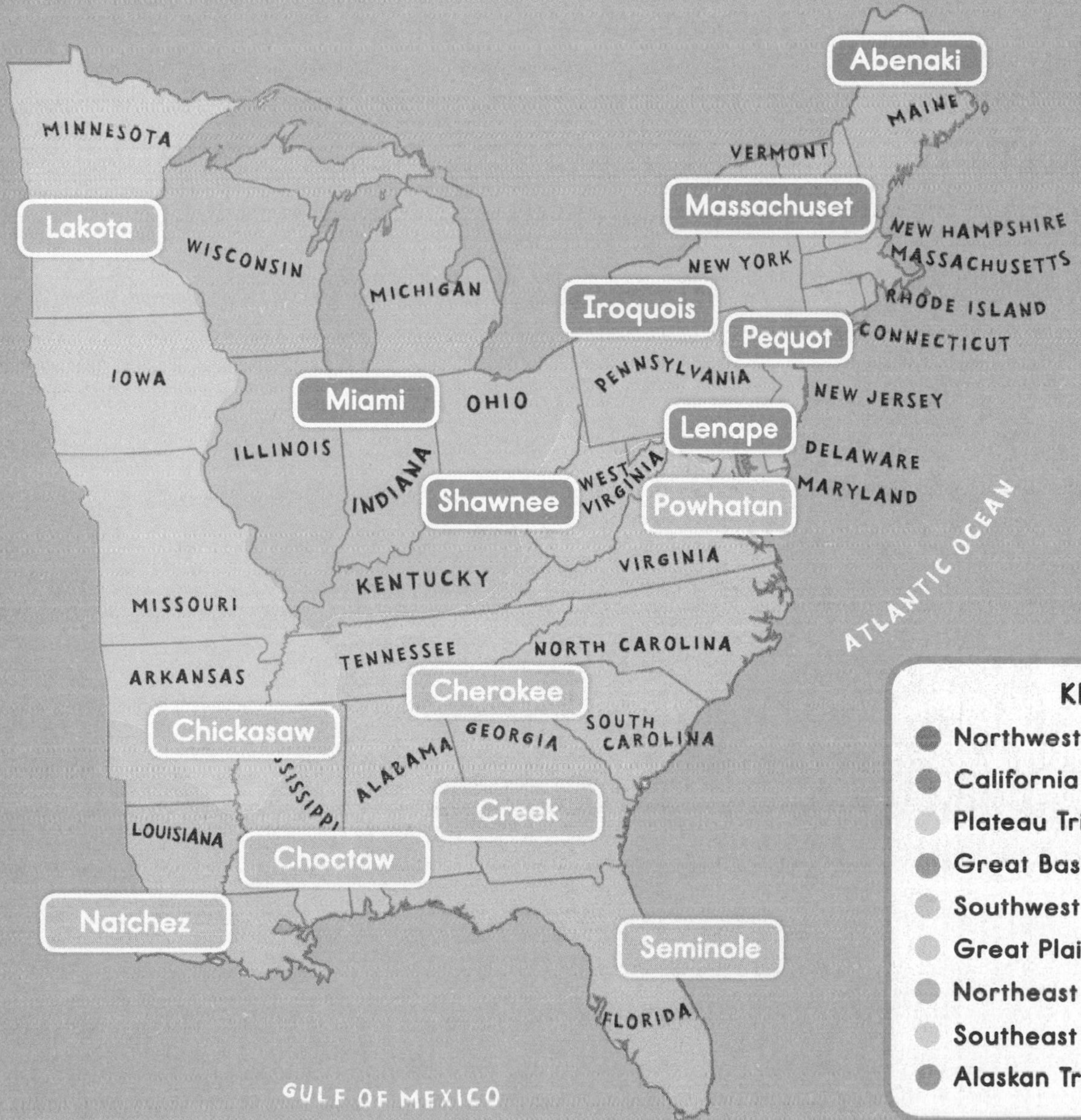

Abenaki
MAINE
VERMONT
Massachuset
MINNESOTA
Lakota
WISCONSIN
NEW HAMPSHIRE
MASSACHUSETTS
NEW YORK
MICHIGAN
Iroquois
RHODE ISLAND
Pequot
CONNECTICUT
PENNSYLVANIA
IOWA
Miami
OHIO
NEW JERSEY
Lenape
ILLINOIS
INDIANA
DELAWARE
WEST VIRGINIA
Shawnee
Powhatan
MARYLAND
ATLANTIC OCEAN
VIRGINIA
KENTUCKY
MISSOURI
TENNESSEE
NORTH CAROLINA
ARKANSAS
Cherokee
Chickasaw
SOUTH CAROLINA
GEORGIA
ALABAMA
MISSISSIPPI
Creek
LOUISIANA
Choctaw
Natchez
Seminole
FLORIDA
GULF OF MEXICO

KEY

- Northwest Coast Tribes
- California Tribes
- Plateau Tribes
- Great Basin Tribes
- Southwest Tribes
- Great Plains Tribes
- Northeast Tribes
- Southeast Tribes
- Alaskan Tribes

Let Me Keep Her!

You found a baby dragon in the woods by the river. Now you must convince your parent to let you keep it. Brainstorm details to support your argument.

Supporting Opinions

What are three facts about dragons that make them a **good** house pet?

Dragons are ______________________________

Dragons can ______________________________

Dragons will never ______________________________

What would be the best part of having a dragon for a pet?

____

What are three facts about dragons that make them a **bad** house pet?

Dragons are ______________________________

Dragons can ______________________________

Dragons will never ______________________________

Brain Box

The goal of **persuasive writing** is to convince the reader to do something or to think a certain way. Persuasive writing uses techniques like highlighting key facts, appealing to the reader's emotions, making an argument, or predicting an outcome.

What would be the worst part of having a dragon for a pet, and how can you avoid this problem?

Supporting Opinions

Using your supporting details, write a paragraph about why you should be able to keep your dragon.

Upon completion, add these stickers to your path on the map!

I should be able to keep my dragon because . . .

BONUS: Besides a dragon, what kind of animal would you like to have for a pet? Give three reasons why that pet is right for you.

Now add this sticker to your map!

Market Math

Color the shapes to show the fraction. Then write the equivalent fraction.

Equivalent Fractions

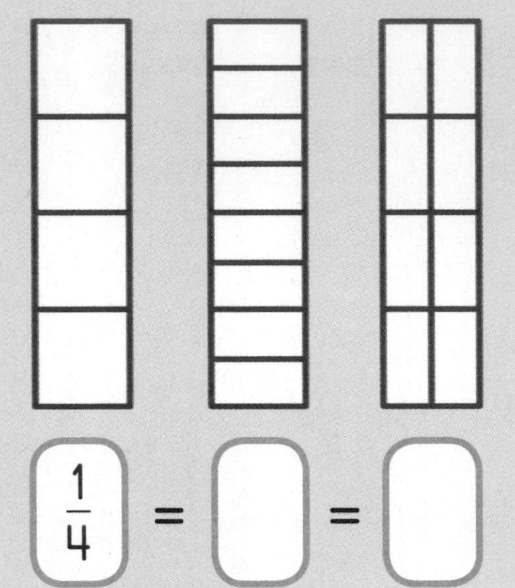

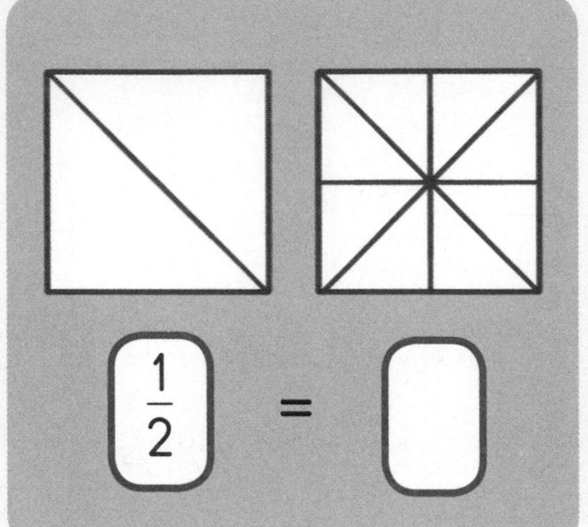

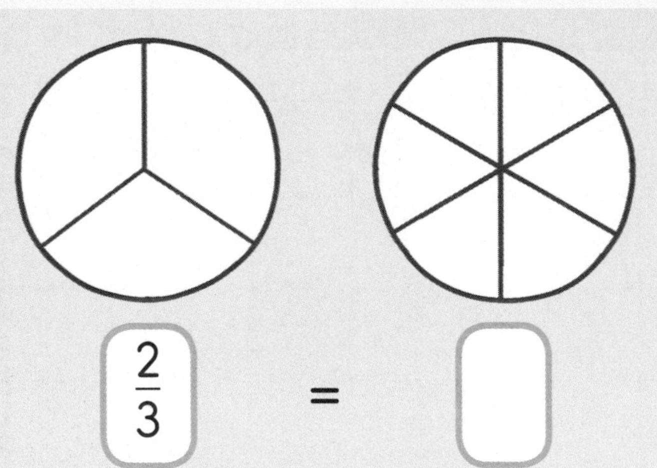

BONUS: Draw a circle and divide it into 8 equal parts. Then draw another circle of the same size and divide it into 4 equal parts. Color parts of each circle so that they show equivalent fractions.

Now add this sticker to your map!

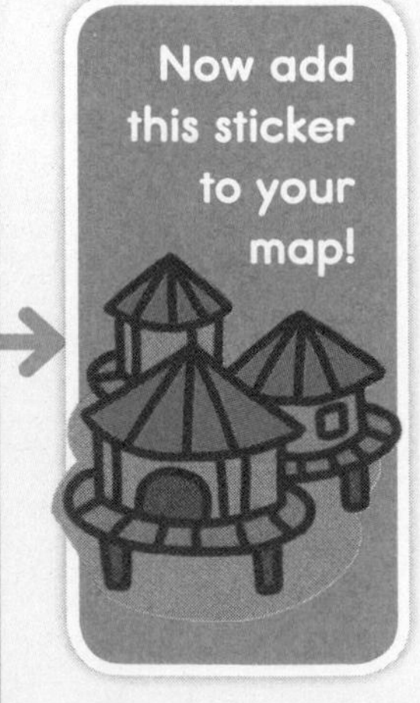

Equivalent Fractions

Answer each question.

Circle the shape that shows a fraction equivalent to $\frac{2}{3}$.

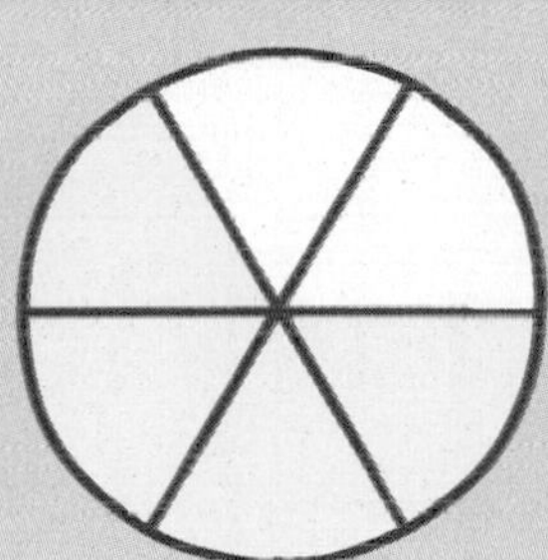

Upon completion, add these stickers to your path on the map!

Do both shapes show $\frac{5}{8}$? Explain why or why not.

____

Circle the shapes that show equivalent fractions. Then write the equivalent fractions.

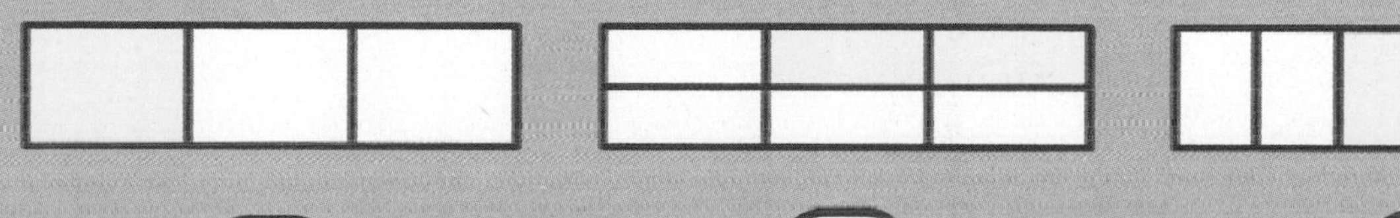

How Does It Feel?

Shades of Meaning

Each pair of words has similar meanings. Circle the word that expresses a more intense feeling. Then use that word in a sentence.

terrified scared

____

happy overjoyed

____

mad furious

____

bothered upset

____

miserable sad

____

thrilled excited

____

exhausted tired

____

few rare

____

Just the Right Word

Complete each sentence in the story by circling the word that fits best.

Shades of Meaning

Brenna always **suspected** **knew** that there were interesting people on the other side of the mountain, but she was never sure. From time to time, travelers would stop by, telling **stories** **fables** about the people they'd met there and how the other side lived. Every time Brenna looked up at the mountain, she **believed** **wondered** what those people on the other side might be like.

Then one day, she decided to climb the mountain. It took her all day to climb up one side and **plummet** **descend** the other. When she came to the other side of the mountain, she met a girl about her own age, named Jenna. Jenna took her home, introduced her to her family, and showed her all around the **village** **country**. Brenna had **heard** **understood** about the people on the other side of the mountain all her life. But now she finally saw them with her own eyes.

Upon completion, add these stickers to your path on the map!

BONUS: Which word best describes a cave with absolutely no light: *dark* or *dim*?

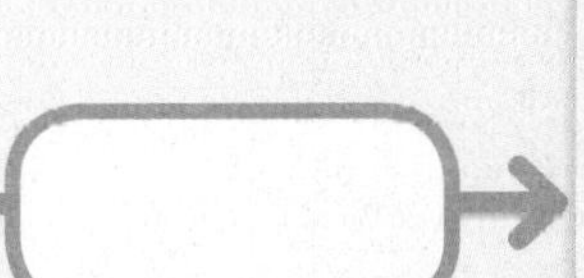

Now add this sticker to your map!

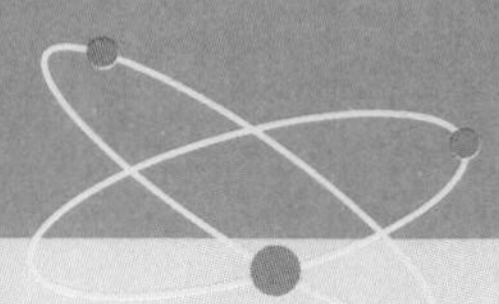

Arrowheads

Fill in the tally chart. Then use the information to complete the dot plot and answer each question.

Data: Dot Plot

ARROWHEAD LENGTH

Length (inches)	$\frac{1}{8}$	$\frac{2}{8}$	$\frac{3}{8}$	$\frac{4}{8}$	$\frac{5}{8}$	$\frac{6}{8}$
Tally	||	|||	~~||||~~ |		||||	|
Number Found	2					

ARROWHEAD LENGTH

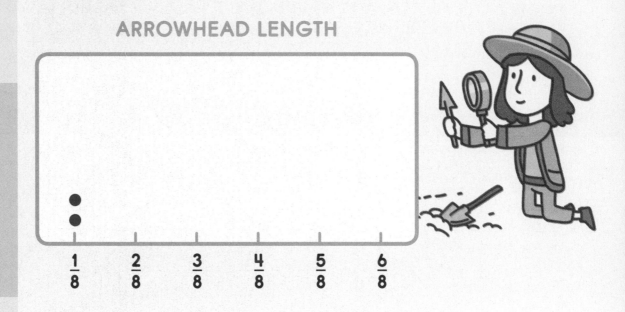

$\frac{1}{8}$ $\frac{2}{8}$ $\frac{3}{8}$ $\frac{4}{8}$ $\frac{5}{8}$ $\frac{6}{8}$

Upon completion, add this sticker to your path on the map!

Which was the most common length of arrowhead?

_____ inch

What size arrowhead was not found?

_____ inch

How many arrowheads were found in total?

_____ arrowheads

Brain Box

A **dot plot** uses a number line to show how many times each number in a set of data occurs. The amount is represented by dots.

Level 5B complete!

Add this achievement sticker to your path...

...and move on to

Level 6

on page 106!

Where Do I Go?

Read the passage.

Habitat and Survival

START LEVEL 6 HERE!

A **habitat** is the environment in which a plant or an animal lives. A habitat includes the other plants and animals in the area, geographic features like soil, beaches, or mountains, and the local weather patterns.

Animals' bodies have adapted to their habitats. Plants and animals that live in the ocean, for instance, have respiratory systems that extract oxygen from the water, rather than the air. Animals that live in very cold environments have heavy coats or layers of fat that keep them insulated from the low temperatures. Plants adapt to different kinds of soil, using the specific minerals to grow strong and healthy.

Some animals can adapt their behavior to survive in a new habitat. Rock doves, for instance, originally built their nests in mountain crevices. Today they make their homes on skyscraper ledges, and most people call them pigeons.

But it's not easy for many animals to change habitats. The heavy fur and layers of fat that keep a polar bear warm in the Arctic Circle would make it very uncomfortable in a tropical climate. And a stalk of seaweed that needs the pressure of water to support its growth will not survive if it's planted on land.

Answer each question using the words in the box.

fur	tentacles	rain	wings	legs

What is one feature that a giant squid lacks to move around on land? ________________

What is one feature that helps a giant squid move around in water? ________________

What is one feature of an eagle that allows it to survive in the forest canopy? ________________

What is one feature of a wolf that would make it hard to survive on a desert island? ________________

What does an evergreen need to survive that it would not get enough of in the desert? ________________

Answer each question.

Why can a rock dove survive in both a mountainous forest and a city environment?

____

____

Would a giant squid survive on land? Why or why not?

____

____

What features help your favorite plant survive in its habitat?

____

____

What features or behaviors help your favorite animal survive in its habitat?

____

____

Upon completion, add these stickers to your path on the map!

Repeating Artifacts

Follow the directions.

Number Patterns

Write the number of feathers in each helmet. Then extend the pattern by writing the next 3 numbers.

____, ____, ____, ____, ____, ____, ____

Describe the pattern.

____

Upon completion, add this sticker to your path on the map!

Complete the pattern by adding 2 repeatedly.

24, ____, ____, ____, ____, ____, ____

Describe the pattern.

____

Complete the pattern by adding 9 repeatedly.

9, ____, ____, ____, ____, ____, ____

Describe the pattern in two different ways.

____

____

Brain Box

To figure out the **pattern** in a series of numbers, look at the relationship between each number and the number that follows.

Example: 5, 10, 15, 20 . . .

5	10	15	20
+5	+5	+5	+5
10	15	20	25

The pattern for this number series is **+5**. The next number in the pattern would be 25.

Living in the Past

What do you think your life would have been like if you had been born 2,000 years earlier? Brainstorm ten adjectives to describe your life and write them in the box. Then write a story describing the events that could have occurred while living in the past. Use your adjectives from the box.

Adjectives

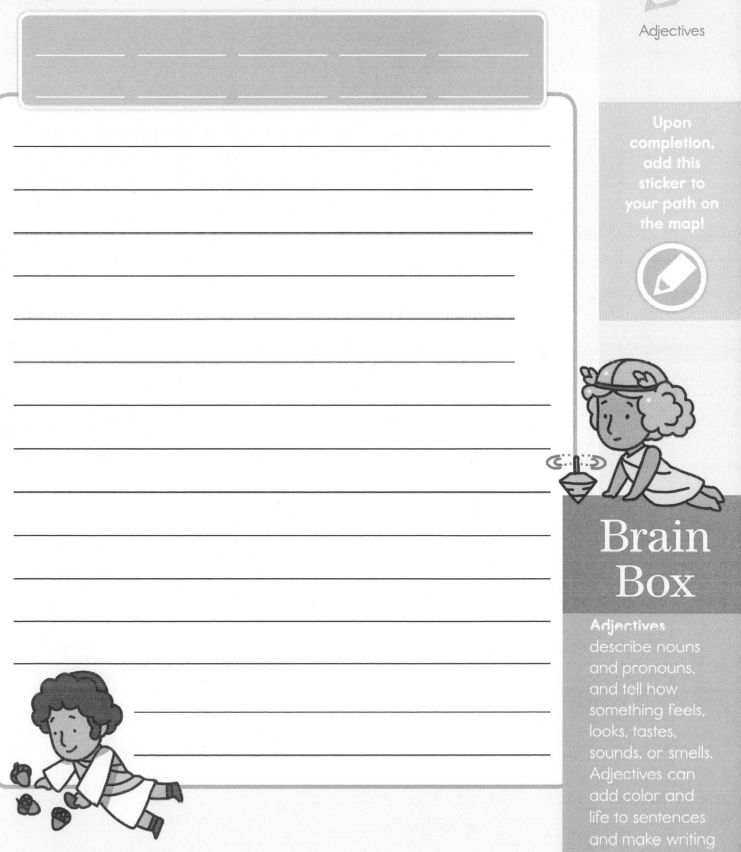

Upon completion, add this sticker to your path on the map!

Brain Box

Adjectives describe nouns and pronouns, and tell how something feels, looks, tastes, sounds, or smells. Adjectives can add color and life to sentences and make writing more interesting.

Foundations of Freedom

Read the article. Then answer each question.

Government

The United States government is made up of three branches. The first is the **legislative branch**, which makes our country's laws. All members of Congress work in this branch. The Congress is divided into two houses: the Senate and the House of Representatives. Each state elects two senators to serve in the Senate, who serve terms of six years. In the House of Representatives, each representative is elected by his or her district and must seek reelection every two years. However, there are no term limits for senators or representatives.

The **executive branch** includes the president and vice president. The president and vice president are elected together for a four-year term. Presidents can serve for a maximum of two terms, or eight years, if they are reelected. The president is the head of the government and the commander in chief of the military. He has the power to sign or veto laws, enforce laws, and propose military action (but only Congress can declare war).

The **judicial branch** is composed of judges and courts. The judges in this branch are appointed by the president and confirmed by Congress. The judges are responsible for interpreting laws and determining if laws are constitutional. The highest court is called the Supreme Court. It has nine judges, called "justices," and they are appointed for life.

This system of government is called a representative democracy—people vote to elect the president and leaders who represent their interests in Congress. It is related to the ancient Greek system of government practiced in the city of Athens. Athenian democracy included the Assembly, which was composed of all citizen voters, who were men over the age of twenty. The Council included 500 men, who handled the day-to-day operations of government. There were courts that handled issues of justice.

Government

How do members of Congress get their jobs?

____

____

The legislative and judicial branches both deal with laws. How are their roles different?

____

____

Upon completion, add these stickers to your path on the map!

Complete the chart using the words and phrases from the box.

legislative	judicial	6 years
2 years	executive	lifetime
interprets laws	makes laws	
enforces laws	4 or 8 years	

Constitution

	House of Representatives	Senate	Supreme Court	President
Branch of government				
Role				
Term of Service				

BONUS: What bodies of government form Congress?

____

____

Now add this sticker to your map!

The Sultan and the Sisters

Read the beginning of this tale from *The Arabian Nights*. Then answer each question.

Understanding Characters

Upon completion, add these stickers to your path on the map!

There was a sultan [emperor] of Persia named Kosrouschah, who, when he first came to his crown, in order to obtain a knowledge of affairs, took great pleasure in night excursions, attended by a trusty minister. He often walked in disguise through the city and met with many adventures, one of the most remarkable of which happened to him upon his first ramble, which was not long after his accession to the throne.

After the ceremonies of his father's funeral rites and his own inauguration, Kosrouschah, from inclination as well as from duty, went out one evening attended by his grand vizier, disguised like himself, to observe what was transacting in the city. As he was passing through a street in the part of the town inhabited only by the meaner sort, he heard some people talking very loudly. Going close to the house whence the noise proceeded, he looked through a crack in the door, perceived a light and three sisters sitting on a sofa, conversing together after supper. By what the eldest said he presently understood the subject of their conversation was wishes: "For," said she, "since we are talking about wishes, mine shall be to have the sultan's baker for my husband, for then I shall eat my fill of that bread, which by way of excellence is called the sultan's; let us see if your tastes are as good as mine." "For my part," replied the second sister, "I wish I was wife to the sultan's chief cook, for then I should eat of the most excellent dishes; and as I am persuaded that the sultan's bread is common in the palace, I should not want any of that; therefore you see," addressing herself to her eldest sister, "that I have a better taste than you." The youngest sister, who was very beautiful, and had more charms and wit than the two elder, spoke in her turn: "For my part, sisters," said she, "I shall not limit my desires to such trifles, but take a higher flight; and since we are upon wishing, I wish to be the emperor's queen-consort. I would make him father of a prince, whose hair should be gold on one side of his head and silver on the other; when he cried, the tears from his eyes should be pearls; and when he smiled, his vermilion lips should look like a rosebud fresh-blown."

The three sisters' wishes, particularly that of the youngest, seemed so singular to the sultan, that he resolved to gratify them in their desires. But without communicating his design to his grand vizier, he charged him only to take notice of the house and bring the three sisters before him the following day.

Understanding Characters

What does the emperor enjoy doing?

____

Do you think the emperor is someone who says everything he's thinking? Why or why not?

____

____

Whom does the first sister say she wants to marry?

____

Why does she want to marry him?

____

Whom does the second sister say she wants to marry?

____

Why does she want to marry him?

____

What are three physical details the third sister uses to describe the son she would like to have?

____

____

Make a prediction. What will the sultan do next?

____

____

____

Brain Box

The people in a work of fiction are called **characters**. You can learn about the characters through their **actions**, **thoughts**, and **speech**.

Survival

Read the passage. Then look at each pair of drawings below and circle the correct answer.

Environment and Characteristics

Animals and plants have features that help them survive in their habitats, like a bird's wings that help it reach its nest in the trees or a giraffe's long neck that helps it eat leaves high on a tree. But environments can change. When they do, the creatures that live in them change too. If there's more food, for instance, animals will grow bigger. If there's less rain, plants won't grow as tall.

Indeed, long-term changes in the environment can cause lasting changes in the plants and animals that live there—the ones that don't adapt struggle to survive, and the ones that do adapt, thrive. Also, variations in characteristics of animals of the same species can provide advantages for surviving, finding mates, and reproducing. For example, a plant with a much larger root system than other plants of the same species may be more likely to survive a drought.

Which of these people had enough to eat when their bones were growing?

Environment and Characteristics

Which of these frogs would be harder for a predator to spot?

Which of these birds would thrive if there were more large seeds to eat than smaller ones?

Upon completion, add these stickers to your path on the map!

Which of these squirrels would survive best if they both had to migrate to a city, where the buildings are mostly gray?

BONUS: What are two factors in a boar's environment that might have caused it to develop tusks?

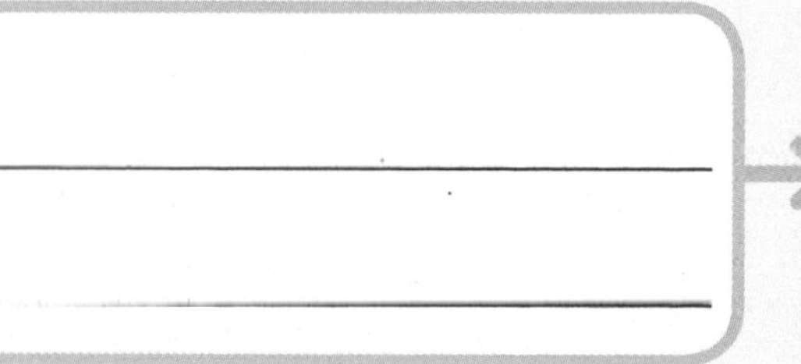

Now add this sticker to your map!

Magical Multiplication

Solve each word problem.

Multiplication Comparisons

An adult dragon has a tail 7 times as long as a baby dragon's tail. If a baby dragon has a tail that is 2 inches, how long is the adult dragon's tail?

7 x 2 = ____ ☐ inches

The wizard's cane is 4 times as long as his apprentice's cane. If the apprentice's cane is 3 feet long, how long is the wizard's cane?

4 x ____ = ____ ☐ feet

The queen's horse runs twice as far as the prince's horse. If the prince's horse runs 10 miles, how far will the queen's horse run?

____ x ____ = ____  miles

Matchups

Draw a line to match each word problem with its equation and solution.

Multiplication and Division

The Loch Ness monster was seen 16 times last year, but only twice this year. How many more times was it seen last year than this year?

$100 \times 7 = n$
$n = 700$

The Cipactli can eat 100 fish in one bite. If it took 7 bites, how many fish could the Cipactli eat?

$9 \times n = 72$
$n = 8$

Upon completion, add these stickers to your path on the map!

The Minotaur frightened 72 villagers this month. This was 9 times as many villagers as last month. How many villagers did the Minotaur frighten last month?

$63 = 7 \times n$
$n = 9$

An Egyptian god had 63 griffins. This was 7 times as many griffins as a Greek god had. How many griffins did the Greek god have?

$16 \div 2 = n$
$n = 8$

Pottery Patterns

Shape Patterns

Look at the patterns below. Then follow the directions.

Circle the smallest set of figures that repeat.

Then draw the next 3 shapes in the pattern.

Circle the smallest set of figures that repeat.

Then draw the next 4 shapes in the pattern.

Upon completion, add this sticker to your path on the map!

Circle the smallest set of figures that repeat.

Then draw the next 5 shapes in the pattern.

BONUS: Draw your own shape pattern for a vase. Use at least 2 different shapes and show a total of 9 shapes. Then describe it in words so someone else could extend it.

Now add this sticker to your map!

Achilles' Heel

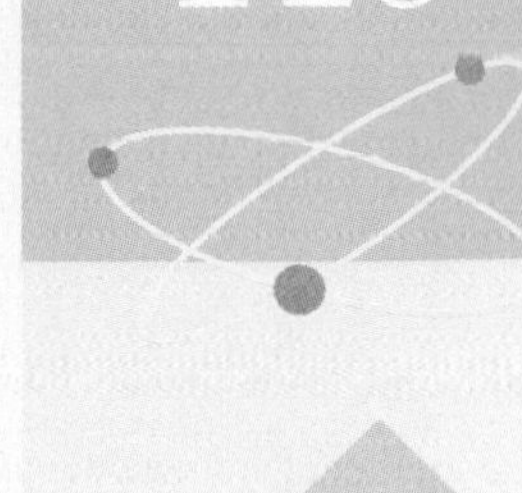

Read the story of Achilles' heel from Greek mythology.

When Achilles was an infant, an oracle warned that he would live only a short life and die young. His mother, Thetis, was distraught, so she took Achilles to the river Styx, which was known for its magical healing powers.

Thetis held her baby by his heel and carefully dipped his entire body into the river to coat him in its enchanted water. He was covered from his head to his toes, but because his mother held his heel, the water didn't touch it.

Achilles grew up and lived a long and eventful life. He fought in many battles, and was a hero of the Trojan War, in which he commanded fifty ships. Throughout many dangerous missions, he was never harmed. At the end of the war, Achilles' rival, Paris, shot a poison arrow directly at his heel—the only part of his body not dipped in the magical river. Achilles fell dead on the spot.

Cause and Effect

Upon completion, add this sticker to your path on the map!

Read each cause and write the effect in a complete sentence.

An oracle warned that Achilles would die young, so ________

____.

Thetis held Achilles by his heel when she dipped him in the river, so ________________________________.

A poison arrow hit Achilles in his unprotected heel, so

____.

Brain Box

Today, the story of Achilles' heel has turned into a saying that is based on the Greek myth. The term is used when someone has a small but disastrous vulnerability despite overall strength. Often that weakness is the **cause** of someone's downfall or misfortune (which is the **effect**), and it is called that person's Achilles' heel.

The Enchanted Types

Read the beginning of "The Enchanted Types," by L. Frank Baum. Then answer each question, using complete sentences.

Narration

One time a Knook became tired of his beautiful life and longed for something new to do.

Finally, by chance, Popopo thought of the earth people who dwell in cities, and so he resolved to visit them and see how they lived.

Therefore, one morning, after a breakfast so dainty that you could scarcely imagine it, Popopo set out for the earth and at once was in the midst of a big city.

His own dwelling was so quiet and peaceful that the roaring noise of the town startled him. His nerves were so shocked that before he had looked around three minutes he decided to give up the adventure, and instantly returned home.

This satisfied for a time his desire to visit the earth cities, but soon the monotony of his existence again made him restless and gave him another thought. At night the people slept and the cities would be quiet. He would visit them at night.

So at the proper time Popopo transported himself in a jiffy to a great city, where he began wandering about the streets.

Everyone was in bed. No wagons rattled along the pavements; no throngs of busy men shouted and halloaed. Even the policemen slumbered slyly and there happened to be no prowling thieves abroad.

His nerves being soothed by the stillness, Popopo began to enjoy himself. He entered many of the houses and examined their rooms with much curiosity. Locks and bolts made no difference to a knook, and he saw as well in darkness as in daylight.

During his wanderings he entered a millinery shop, and was surprised to see within a large glass case a great number of women's hats, each bearing in one position or another a stuffed bird. Indeed, some of the most elaborate hats had two or three birds upon them.

Now, knooks are the especial guardians of birds and love them dearly. To see so many of his little friends shut up in a glass case annoyed

and grieved Popopo, who had no idea they had purposely been placed upon the hats by the milliner.

So he slid back one of the doors of the case, gave the little chirruping whistle of the knooks that all birds know well, and called: "Come, friends; the door is open—fly out!"

Popopo did not know the birds were stuffed; but, stuffed or not, every bird is bound to obey a knook's whistle and a knook's call. So they left the hats, flew out of the case and began fluttering about the room.

"Poor dears!" said the kindhearted knook, "you long to be in the fields and forests again."

Then he opened the outer door for them and cried: "Off with you! Fly away, my beauties, and be happy again."

Upon completion, add these stickers to your path on the map!

How is the city different from Popopo's life at home?

____

What are three details that describe the city at night?

____

Many of the paragraphs in this story begin with a word or phrase that helps us understand the sequence of events. Make a list of those words or phrases, in the order they appear.

____

____

Underline the last sentence of dialogue in this story. What does it tell you about Popopo?

____

____

Make a prediction. What will happen the next morning when the residents of the city wake up?

____

____

____

____

CONGRATULATIONS!
You completed all of your reading and writing quests! You earned:

World Heroes

Read about each historical figure.

Historical Figures

ABRAHAM LINCOLN was president of the United States from 1861 to 1865, during the Civil War. He led the fight to preserve the Union. He was certain that the South should not secede and form its own country. He signed the Emancipation Proclamation, which allowed both free and enslaved African Americans to join the Union army and made slavery a more central cause of the war. As a result, when the Union won, people who had been living in slavery were free.

MAHATMA GANDHI successfully led the movement for India's independence from the British Empire using nonviolent tactics. Under his leadership, large numbers of India's people participated in civil disobedience by refusing to work, sitting in the streets, or boycotting the courts. Britain agreed to give India its freedom in 1947.

In 1955, **ROSA PARKS** refused to give up her seat on the bus to a white passenger and was arrested. This event served as the spark for the Montgomery bus boycott, during which African American customers refused to ride the buses until they were given the same rights as white passengers. Her act was a major turning point in the civil rights movement that ended legal segregation in the United States.

CRAZY HORSE was a leader of the Oglala Lakota, who fought for the right of his people to remain free on their own land. His war party played an important role in defeating General George Custer at the Battle of Little Big Horn in 1876. Despite this military victory, the United States government ultimately had more resources; in 1877 the Lakota and other Native American tribes lost their land and were forced to relocate to reservations.

MARIE CURIE was a Polish scientist who was a pioneer in the field of physics and chemistry, and also challenged society's thoughts of what women could do. She won the Nobel Prize twice—in 1903 and 1911—for her research on radioactivity and the discovery of the two elements polonium and radium. Her contributions to science led to a treatment for cancer, the study of the atom, and more.

Compare and contrast the paired historical figures. Then write what they all have in common.

Similarity: ______________________________

____

Difference: ______________________________

____

Similarity: ______________________________

____

Difference: ______________________________

____

Similarity: ______________________________

____

Difference: ______________________________

____

Similarity: ______________________________

____

Difference: ______________________________

____

SOMETHING THEY ALL HAVE IN COMMON ______________________________

____

____

Upon completion, add these stickers to your path on the map!

CONGRATULATIONS!
You completed all of your social studies quests! You earned:

Winged Wonders

Solve the word problems.

Multi-Step Word Problems

Poseidon saw 3 groups of 12 flying horses. Sixteen of the horses were blue and the rest were white. How many flying horses were white?

3 × 12 = 36 − 16 = white flying horses

Harpies stole 4 bags of food from a village and 9 bags of food from traveling minstrels. Each bag had 6 sandwiches in it. How many sandwiches did the harpies steal?

sandwiches

Odysseus battled 4 groups of 7 centaurs and 2 groups of 8 centaurs. If he captured all centaurs and divided them equally into 4 cages, how many centaurs would be in each cage?

centaurs

BONUS: Write a word problem about Hermes' winged shoes that takes two steps to solve. Then write the equation and answer.

Now add this sticker to your map!

A sphinx knows 156 different riddles, but travelers solved 132 of the riddles. The sphinx divided the remaining riddles evenly into easy and hard categories. How many riddles were in each group?

Multi-Step Word Problems

☐ riddles

Hermes flew 200 miles to deliver a message to the Greek gods. Then he made short trips of 10 miles each. If he flew 250 miles in all, how many trips did he take?

☐ trips

Upon completion, add these stickers to your path on the map!

Hermes has 25 golden winged hats and twice as many silver winged hats. How many winged hats does he have in all?

☐ winged hats

CONGRATULATIONS!
You completed all of your math quests! You earned:

Harness Your Power

Label each picture with a word from the box. Then circle each paragraph that describes a renewable source of energy.

Natural Fuels

wind	hydro	solar	natural gas	coal

_______________ power comes from the energy released when coal is burned. The raw coal is mined from deposits buried in the earth.

Upon completion, add this sticker to your path on the map!

_______________ power captures the energy of the sun, through panels that absorb sunshine and turn it into energy that can be used as electrical power in homes and businesses.

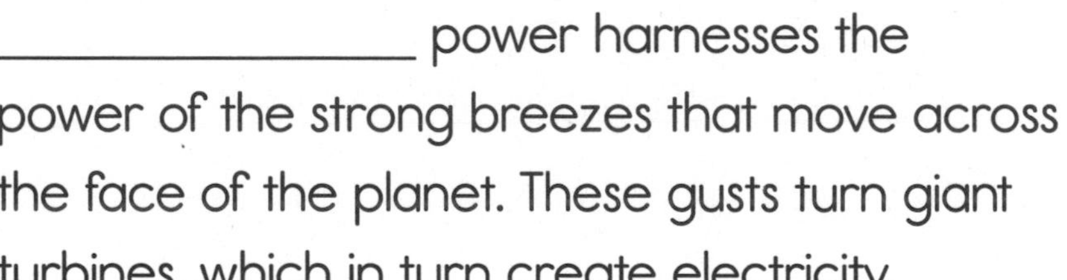

_______________ power harnesses the power of the strong breezes that move across the face of the planet. These gusts turn giant turbines, which in turn create electricity.

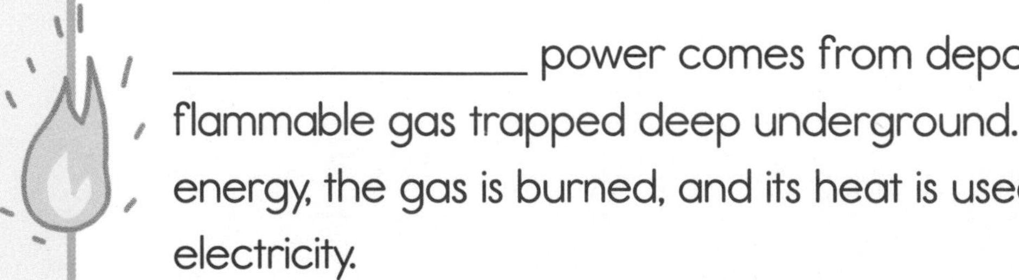

_______________ power comes from deposits of flammable gas trapped deep underground. To release the energy, the gas is burned, and its heat is used to generate electricity.

_______________ power comes from the force of water rushing over dams that are built to contain the flow of a river. The power of the water turns giant turbines, which in turn create electricity.

CONGRATULATIONS!
You completed all of your science quests! You earned:

Quest complete!

Add this achievement sticker to your path…

QUEST
complete!
Welcome to
4th grade!

…and turn to the next page for your Summer Brainiac Award!

Summer Brainiac Award!

You have completed your entire Summer Brain Quest! Woo-hoo! Congratulations! That's quite an achievement.

Write your name on the line and cut out the award certificate. Show your friends. Hang it on your wall! You're a certified Summer Brainiac!

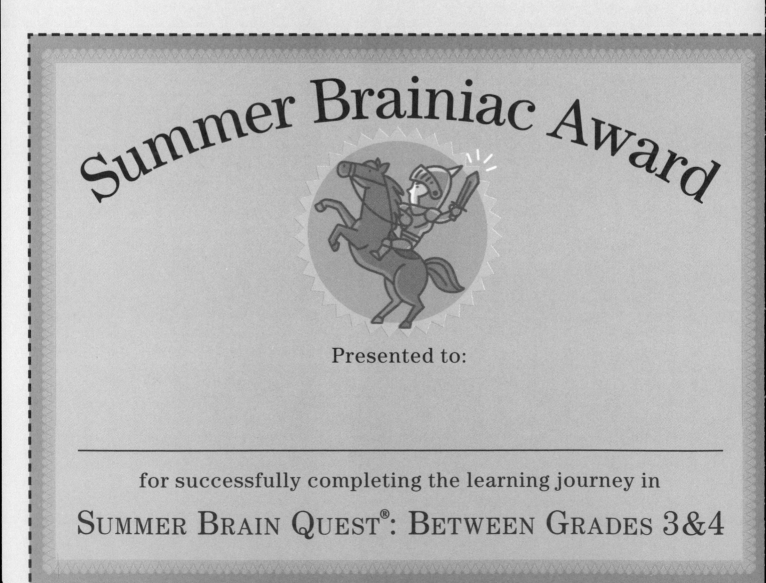

Summer Brainiac Award

Presented to:

____

for successfully completing the learning journey in

SUMMER BRAIN QUEST®: BETWEEN GRADES 3&4

Outside Quests

This is not just a workbook—it's a voyage at sea, a hike in the wild, a way to enjoy the summer sunshine, and so much more! Summer is the perfect time to explore the great outdoors. Use the Outside Quests to make your next sunny day more fun than ever—and earn an achievement sticker.

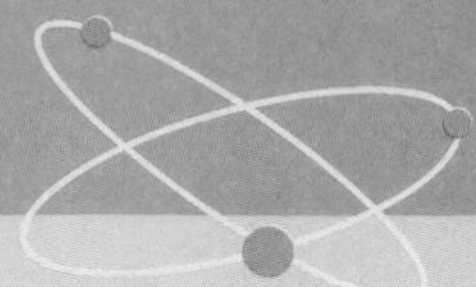

Level 2 Jumping Rhymes

Get a jump rope and a partner. Choose a word and begin jumping rope. Every time the rope hits the ground, say a word that rhymes with your chosen word. Have your partner count the number of rhyming words you say while jumping rope. Next, it's your partner's turn—but he or she can't repeat any of the words you've already said. See who can make the most rhymes.

Now add this sticker to your map!

Level 3B Mayor for a Day

Go to a park, a local historic building, or a shoreline of a lake or river. What is the resource that this location has to offer the community? What are the problems and benefits with this resource? Perform some research—interview employees, walk the grounds, or read about it at your local library. Then write a short proposal for how you would improve the location to better benefit the community.

Now add this sticker to your map!

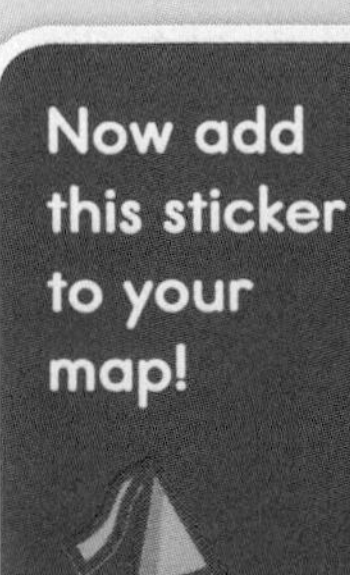

Survival Skills

Go outside and spot an animal. Make a list of what that animal needs to survive. Then explore your neighborhood until you find where it might get each item it needs to survive, such as water from a puddle and shelter in a tree.

Now add this sticker to your map!

Chalky Challenge

Get three different colors of chalk. Draw a rectangle and divide it into 8 equal parts. Color a few of the parts of the rectangle in one color. Color a few of the remaining parts in a second color. Then color the rest of the parts in the third color. Then name the fraction of the rectangle that is in each color. Next try it with a rectangle divided into 10 equal parts. (You can also play this with one or two partners—each player can have their own color of chalk.)

$\frac{4}{8}$ $\frac{1}{8}$ $\frac{3}{8}$

Now add this sticker to your map!

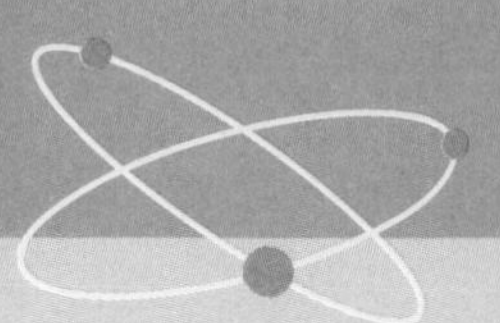

Level 5A Wild Stories

Go outside and look for an animal. When you see one, write down a few lines about the animal, what it is doing, and what it may be thinking. Then write a one-page story that continues from that point, including description, detail, and dialogue.

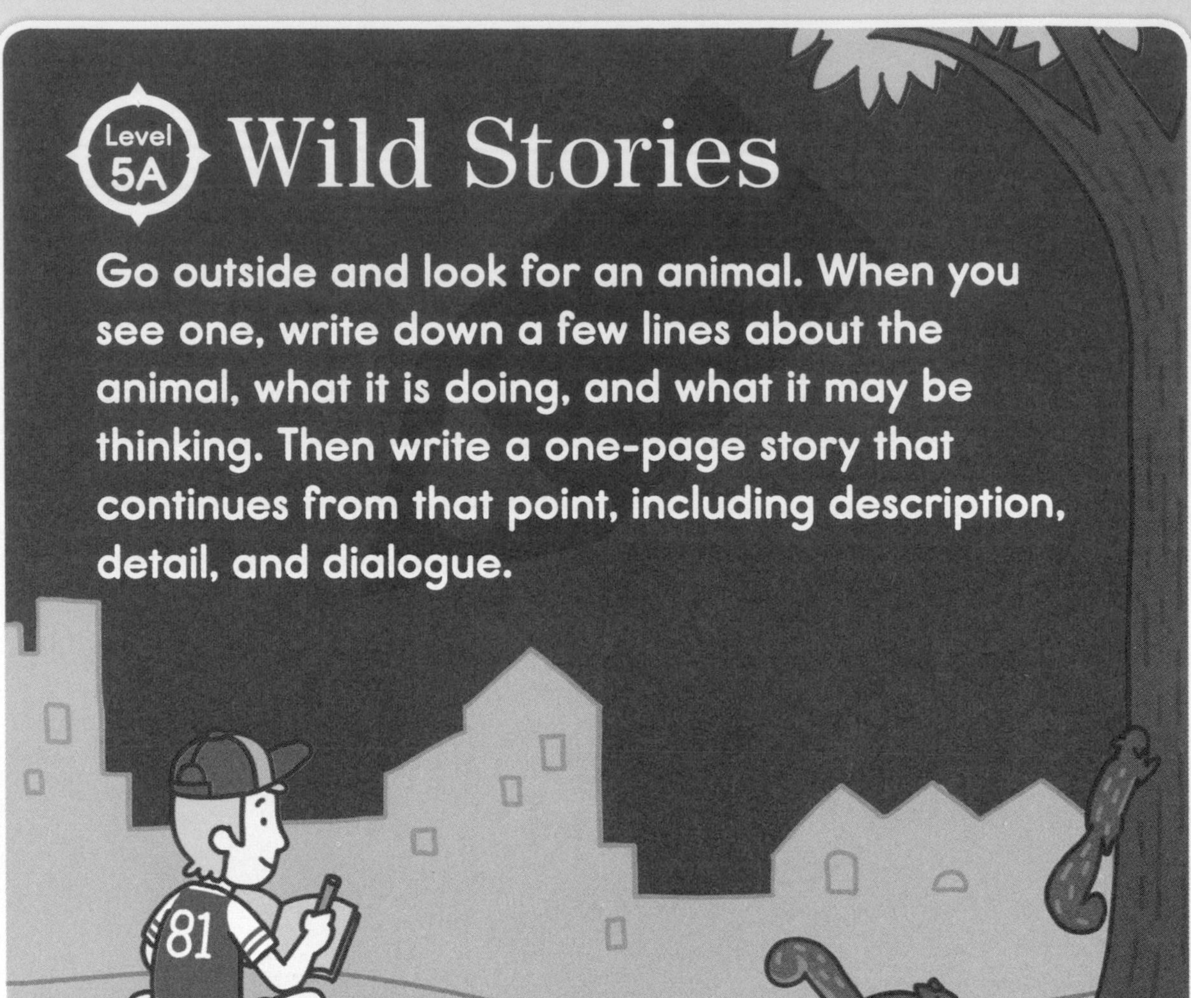

Now add this sticker to your map!

Level 5B Nature's Patterns

Find a partner. Collect groups of natural objects, like rocks, leaves, or flowers. Use two different items to make a pattern such as rock, leaf, rock, leaf, rock, leaf, and have your partner continue the pattern that you began. Now it's your partner's turn to make a pattern. To make the game more difficult, use three or more items to make a pattern such as rock, flower, leaf, rock, flower, leaf. Continue to extend the number of objects in your patterns.

Now add this sticker to your map!

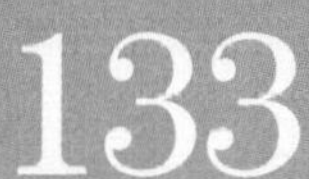

Compare and Contrast

Go to a local event, like a game, concert, or street fair. Ask two attendees what they think about it. Make a chart to compare and contrast what they agreed on and what they disagreed about.

Now add this sticker to your map!

Objects in Motion

Take two balls outside, one large and one small, and find a hill to roll them down. See which one rolls the farthest. Why do you think that is?

Next, find a flat piece of pavement, and roll the big ball into the small ball, and then the small one into the big one. See which one knocks the other one farthest. Why do you think that is?

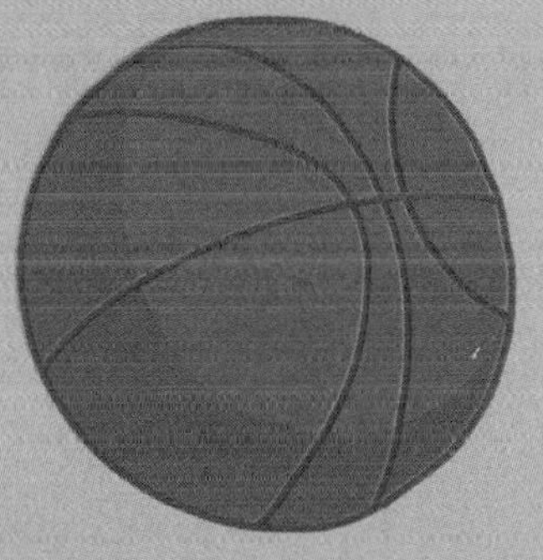

Now add this sticker to your map!

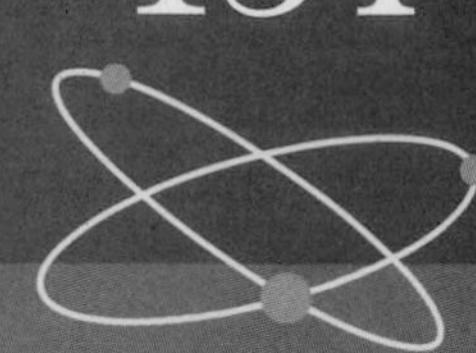

Answer Key

(For pages not included in this section, answers will vary.)

LEVEL 1

page 10

One of the first ways people traveled the world was by sea.

Fragment: Answers will vary. Sample: They canoed and sailed to discover new lands or escape trouble at home.

Run-on: Answers will vary. Sample: Ancient people crossed vast seas and oceans in all sorts of dugout vessels. They were driven by commerce, conflict, and climate, like seasonal changes in wild plants and game.

Fragment: Answers will vary. Sample: From one side of the ocean to the other, ancient people exchanged technology, new ways of thinking, agriculture, and arts.

Today, people still cross oceans for many of the same reasons: climate change, political upheaval, and to find a better life.

page 11

Inland:	**Oceanside:**
seaweed	bananas
fish	logs

Answers will vary. Sample: Each community could trade with the other community.

page 12

100	400	600	700
900	800	500	800
130	420	760	930
440	220	510	360

245, 246, 247, 248, 249, 250, 251, 252, 253, 254

page 13

page 14

underwater: below the surface of water
invisible: not visible
unbelievable: not believable
disagree: don't agree
powerful: full of power
sailor: someone who sails
impossible: not possible
BONUS: est

page 15

primary
primary
secondary
secondary
primary

pages 16–17

dolphin
pelican
seaside moth
Answers will vary.

BONUS:

adolescent

child

adult

infant

page 18

6 × 3 = 18
3 × 8 = 24
4 × 7 = 28
5 × 4 = 20
2 × 9 = 18

LEVEL 2

pages 20–21

Amon (is) the ancient Egyptian king of the gods.
Amon was the ancient Egyptian king of the gods.
Mut, or Mother, (wears) two crowns, one for Upper Egypt and one for Lower Egypt.
Mut, or Mother, wore two crowns, one for Upper Egypt and one for Lower Egypt.
Ancient Egyptians (believe) that Ra, God of the Sun, (is) reborn every day.
Ancient Egyptians believed that Ra, God of the Sun, was reborn every day.
The Opet Festival (is) a boat parade that (brings) statues of three gods to the temple of Luxor.
The Opet Festival was a boat parade that brought statues of three gods to the temple of Luxor.
Osiris, God of Transition, (is) shown with green skin, to remind people of the fields that grow after the floods.
Osiris, God of Transition, was shown with green skin, to remind people of the fields that grow after the floods.
Mice (cause) such a problem in Egypt that cats (have) their own goddess, Bastet.
Mice caused such a problem in Egypt that cats had their own goddess, Bastet.
Geb, God of the Earth, (wears) a goose on his head.
Geb, God of the Earth, wore a goose on his head.
Ancient Egyptians (believe) the earth (shakes) whenever Geb (laughs.)
Ancient Egyptians believed the earth shook whenever Geb laughed.
Ancient Egyptians (don't) celebrate the New Year on any particular date, but (hold) gatherings and feasts whenever the floods (come.)
Ancient Egyptians didn't celebrate the New Year on any particular date, but held gatherings and feasts whenever the floods came.
BONUS: was; became; bound; took

page 22

The empire expanded.

Answers will vary. Sample: The people had peace and prosperity.

Any four of the following: Palaces, cities, places of worship, education, and the arts.

Yes, education was important to Mansa Musa. This was shown in his decision to build a university in Timbuktu.

Answers will vary. Sample: Mansa Musa's decisions improved people's lives for years to come. They enjoyed cities and access to education.

page 23

The wagon that is moving faster will be harder to stop because the higher an object's speed, the more work it takes to stop the object.

The larger rock will be harder to stop because objects with a larger mass require more work to stop once they are moving.

When the shooter's marble hits the other marbles, the shooter's marble will come to a stop. The other marble that has been hit will begin moving.

pages 24–25

4 × 6 = 24
3 × 9 = 27
4 × 8 = 32
7 × 5 = 35
6 × 6 = 36
5 × 8 = 40
8 × 6 = 48
5 × 6 = 30

BONUS: Answers will vary but can include:
1 row of 12 for 1 × 12 = 12
12 rows of 1 for 12 × 1 = 12
2 rows of 6 for 2 × 6 = 12
6 rows of 2 for 6 × 2 = 12
3 rows of 4 for 3 × 4 = 12
4 rows of 3 for 4 × 3 = 12

page 26

constructed
grew
built
cooked
baked
mine
get
were
mixed
dragged

page 27

So that he could eat his entire lunch by himself while Turtle was away

Turtle felt tricked and wanted to get even.

I believe that Anansi knew he was not being a good friend to Turtle. He said early in this story that he did not want to share, and then he tricked his friend.

He felt tricked.

page 28

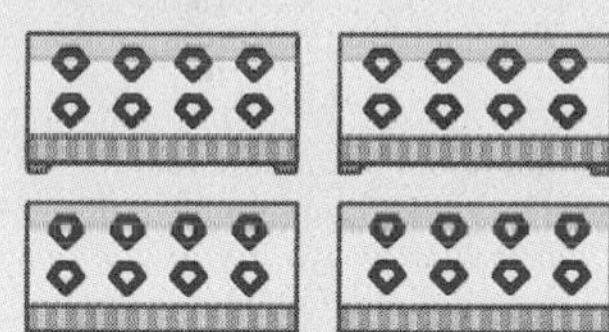

32 ÷ 4 = 8

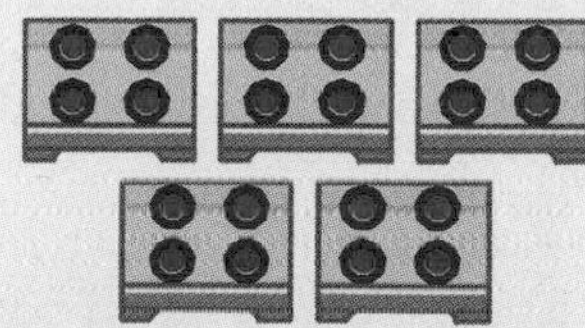

20 ÷ 5 = 4

21 ÷ 3 = 7

18 ÷ 2 = 9

LEVEL 3A

page 31

Poseidon offered the people seawater.

Athena offered the people an olive tree.

Seawater is not good for drinking, washing, or watering plants.

Olive trees provide olives, olive oil, and olive wood.

The main idea of the story is that Athena gave a better gift. Answers will vary. Sample: We know this because the people of the city chose Athena as their defender based on her gift.

Athena's gift was the better gift because it provided the most useful benefits to the people of the city. We know this because the story states that the olive tree she gave the city offered fruits to eat, oil to use, and beautiful wood.

page 32

above
on
in front of
beside/next to
Answers will vary:
under/below/underneath

page 33

Alex likes to read and learn new things.

Chloe would rather have an imperfect version of something than risk having nothing at all.

Daphne knows that words can hurt people's feelings.

page 34

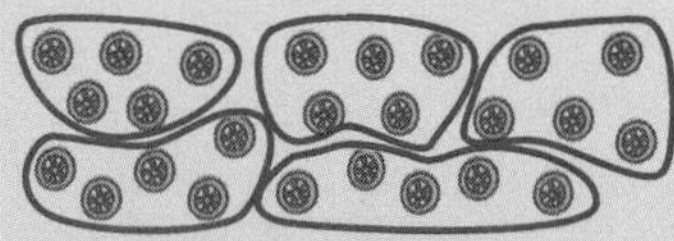

25 ÷ 5 = 5

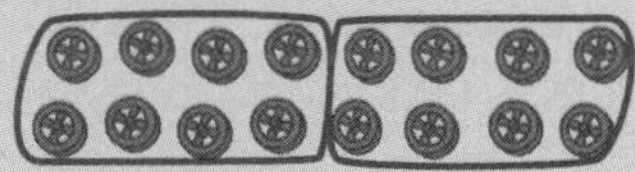

16 ÷ 8 = 2

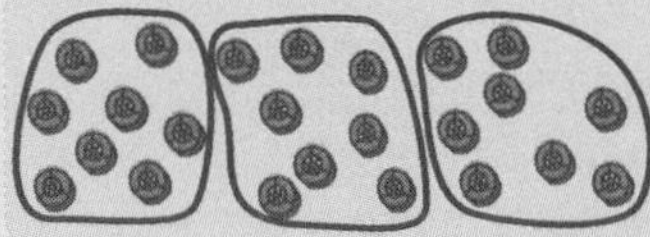

24 ÷ 8 = 3

5 + 2 + 3 = 10

page 35

sandbags
hedges and windbreaks
lightning rods
BONUS: Answers will vary.

pages 36–37

5
3
1
4
6
2

page 38

6 × 2 = 12
12 × 1 = 12
7 × 8 = 56
10 × 4 = 40
BONUS: Answers will vary. Sample: The monster has 4 paws. How many paws will 6 monsters have in all?

page 39

A year on Mars is 687 days.

It is winter in Los Angeles in January because the northern hemisphere is tilted away from the sun.

It is summer in Canberra in January because the southern hemisphere is tilted toward the sun.

The seasons depend on whether the earth is tilted toward or away from the sun.

page 40

north / northwest
Antandrus
Sestus and Elaeus
Sestus
Troy to Lyrnessus
BONUS: Turkey

page 41

when
who
why
whose
whom
that
where

page 42

40 ÷ 8 = 5
48 ÷ 6 = 8
42 ÷ 6 = 7
18 ÷ 2 = 9
28 ÷ 4 = 7

LEVEL 3B

page 44

5 × 2 = **10**
So 2 × **5** = **10**
Commutative property

3 × 4 × 2 = (3 × 4) × **2**
= **12** × 2
= **24**
Associative property

9 × 6 = **54**
So 6 × **9** = **54**
Commutative property

page 45

10 × 7 = **70**
So **7** × 10 = **70**
Commutative property

8 × 7 = 8 × (2 + 5)
= (8 × **2**) + (8 × 5)
= **16** + **40**
= **56**
Distributive property

4 × 2 × 5 = 4 × (2 × **5**)
= 4 × **10**
= **40**
Associative property

5 × 9 = 5 × (6 + 3)
= (5 × **6**) + (5 × **3**)
= **30** + **15**
= **45**
Distributive property

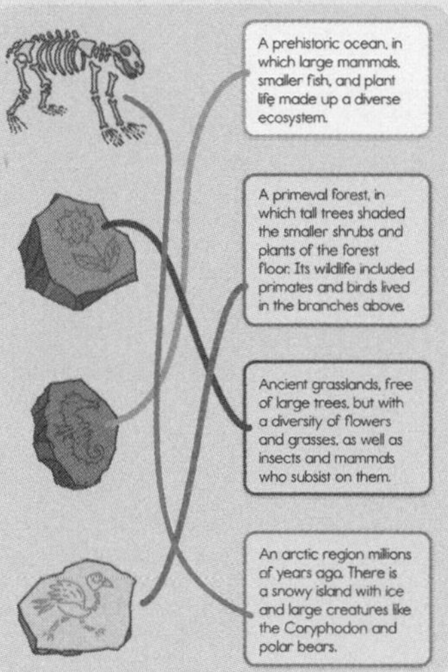

page 47

China
Rome
tea, sugar, salt, spices, and porcelain
language and disease

The Silk Road became less important in the fifteenth century because new direct sea routes were discovered that replaced the Silk Road.

pages 48–49

asked
him
he
get
happened
went
these
pushed
they
ran
have
lives
has
his

page 50

page 51

BECAUSE SHE DIDN'T SEE THE POINT
BONUS: Answers will vary. Samples: 400 + 113 = 513; 796 – 283 = 513

page 52

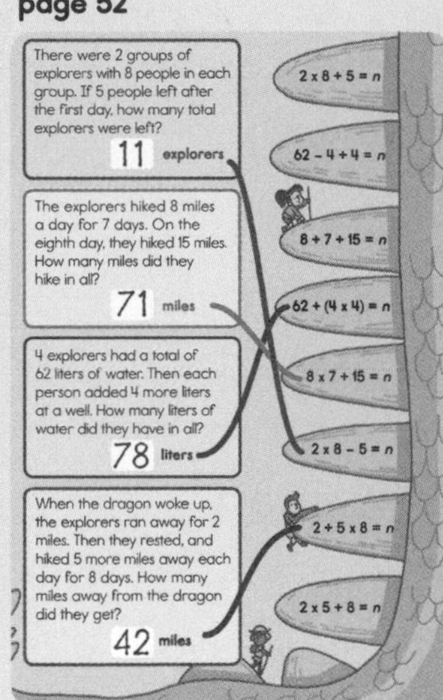

page 53

bigger
smart
fastest
darker
old
brightest

short
Answers will vary.
quick
Answers will vary.
smelly
Answers will vary.

page 54

page 55

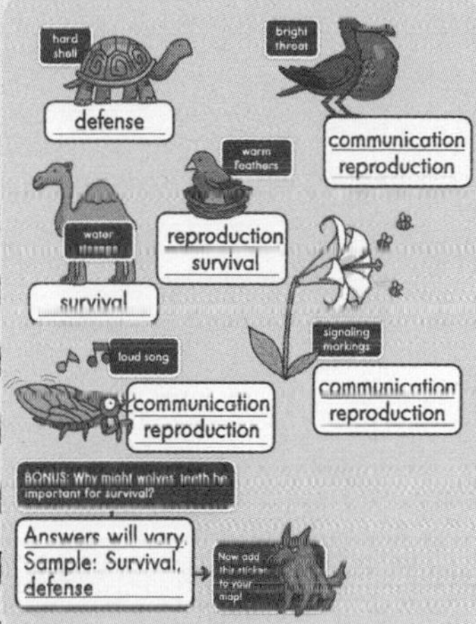

page 56

were
was
had
were
was
was

LEVEL 4A

page 58

simple
complex
complex
compound
compound
complex

page 59

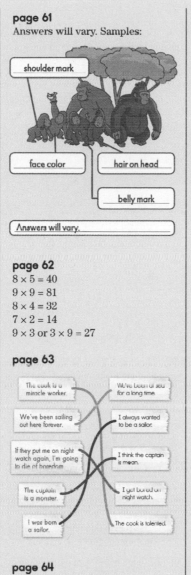

coordinating
subordinating
coordinating
subordinating
subordinating

page 60

A ton of bronze is more difficult to carry or transport than coins.

A year of labor takes a longer time to pay than coins.

A parcel of land can't be moved or transported as easily as coins.

Produce won't last as long as coins.

BONUS: 90¢

page 61

Answers will vary. Samples:

page 62

$8 \times 5 = 40$
$9 \times 9 = 81$
$8 \times 4 = 32$
$7 \times 2 = 14$
9×3 or $3 \times 9 = 27$

page 63

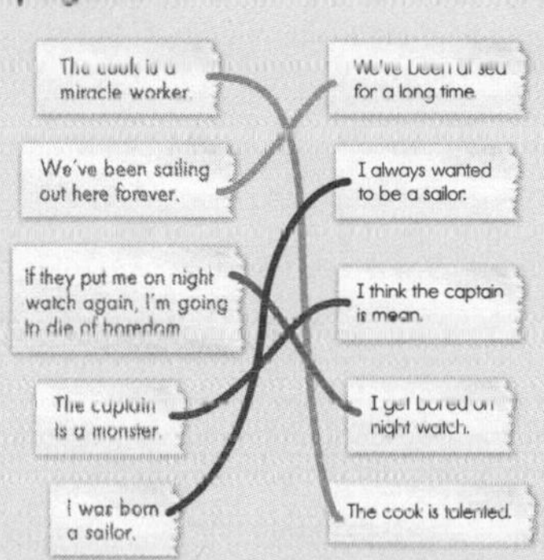

The cook is a miracle worker.
We've been sailing out here forever.
If they put me on night watch again, I'm going to die of boredom.
The captain is a monster.
I was born a sailor.
We've been at sea for a long time.
I always wanted to be a sailor.
I think the captain is mean.
I get bored on night watch.
The cook is talented.

page 64

lunar new year celebrations happen every year starting on the night before the year ends

family members will clean each familys house to sweep away bad fortune

people greet each other by saying things like peace all year round

on the first day of the celebration fireworks are set off to chase away bad spirits

the holiday is celebrated in many asian countries and asian communities all around the world

the lunar new years last celebration is the lantern festival

to celebrate people light lanterns of all kinds including some that float away on lakes or streams

page 65

every
celebrates
clothes
Then
roofs
knowledge
BONUS: their, cities, because

page 66

$4 + 3 + 4 + 3$ or $2 \times 4 + 2 \times 3$ or $2(4 + 3)$; 14
$5 + 1 + 5 + 1$ or $2 \times 5 + 2 \times 1$ or $2(5 + 1)$; 12
$8 + 8 + 8$ or 3×8; 24
2

LEVEL 4B

page 68

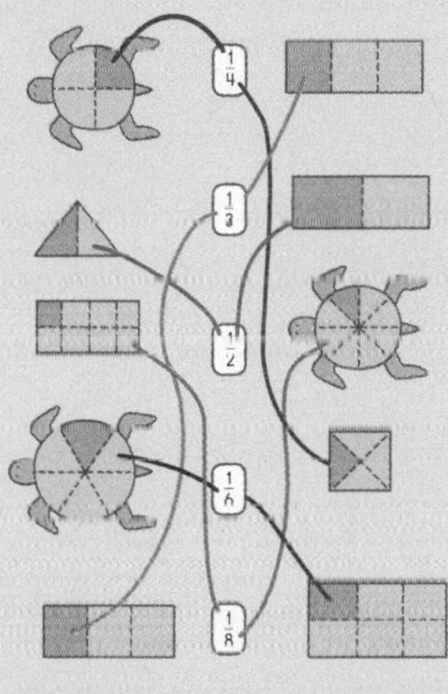

page 69

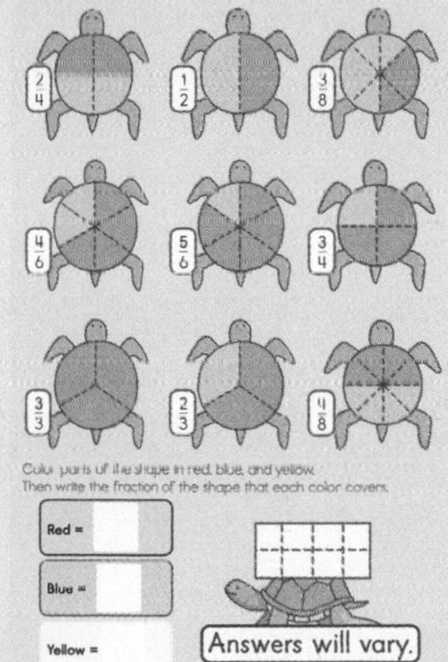

page 70

help them get along
protect the group
care for the infant
hunt together
sharing knowledge
BONUS: to reproduce

page 71

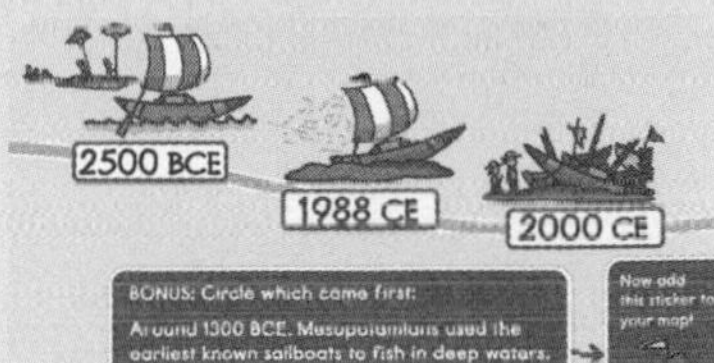

2500 BCE
1988 CE
2000 CE
BONUS: Circle which came first:
Around 1300 BCE, Mesopotamians used the earliest known sailboats to fish in deep waters.
Around 4000 BCE, Egyptians came up with the idea of attaching a sail to a simple boat.

page 72

quite, quiet
Are, our
Then, than
two, to, too
bald, bawled

page 73

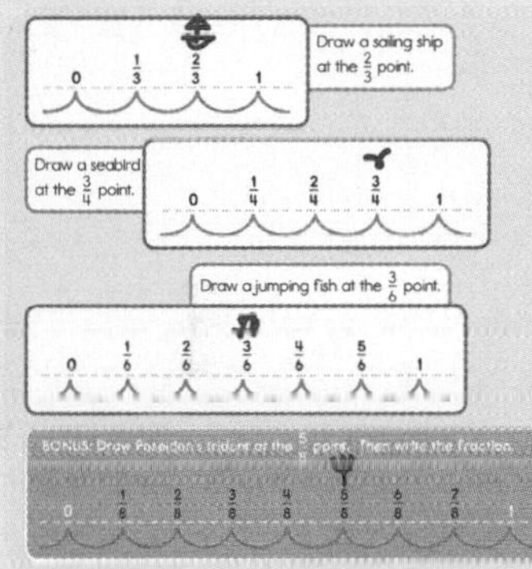

Draw a sailing ship at the 2/3 point.
Draw a seabird at the 3/4 point.
Draw a jumping fish at the 3/6 point.

page 74

$\frac{3}{4} > \frac{2}{4}$

$\frac{4}{6} < \frac{5}{6}$

$\frac{3}{8} < \frac{5}{8}$

$\frac{1}{3} < \frac{2}{3}$

page 75

$\frac{2}{8} < \frac{3}{4}$

$\frac{1}{3} < \frac{5}{6}$

$\frac{3}{4} > \frac{3}{8}$

$\frac{1}{2} > \frac{1}{6}$

page 76

change direction
damage
sailor
ship that gets ahead of others
tool that measures latitude

LEVEL 5A

page 78

poem
prose
drama
BONUS: poetry

page 79

capital
human
natural
human
Answers will vary.

page 80
6; 6
$6 + 6 = 12$; 12
$12 \div 3 = 4$; 4
3; 5; 2
$3 + 5 + 2 = 10$; 10
$10 \div 5 = 2$; 2

page 81
Answers will vary.
BONUS: It would cut down on waste.

page 82

parallelograms	rectangles	quadrilaterals
parallelogram	rectangle	square
square	square	rectangle
rectangle		rhombus
rhombus		parallelogram
		trapezoid

page 83
Answers will vary. Samples:

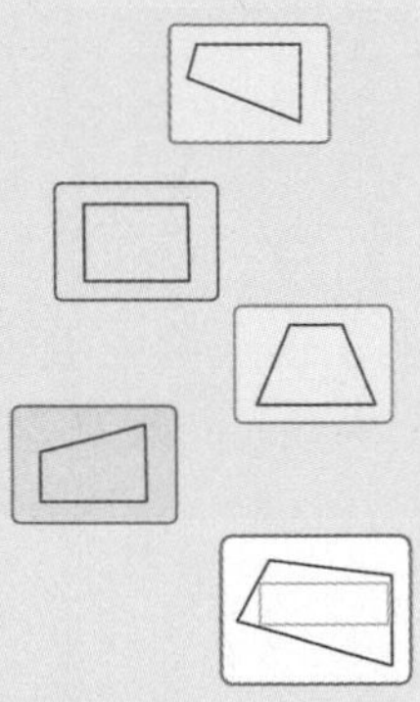

page 87
it sparkles in the sunset and the books on the bookshelves
the strange carvings
the turquoise mask of the queen
a few small boxes of coins and jewelry
the books in the library
BONUS: Sara would be interested in the scrolls. John would be interested in the treasure. Answers will vary.

page 88
4
cat
26
2
4

page 89
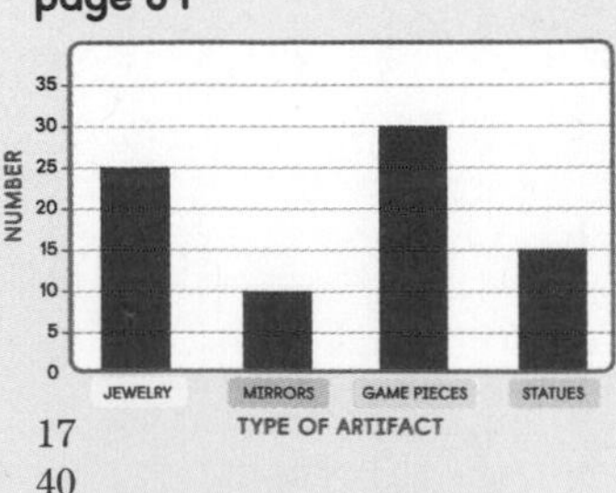

17
40
It would appear between the lines for 15 and 20 but closer to the line for 15.

page 90
flour
oil
They are golden brown on both sides.
No, because you would miss steps in the process.
No, because the steps would be out of order.

LEVEL 5B

page 92

Answers will vary.
Answers will vary.

page 93
5:08 a.m.
8:43 a.m.
11:54 a.m.
2:45 p.m.
7:11 p.m.
8:32 p.m.

page 94
9:30 a.m.
9:48 a.m.
29
54
BONUS: 1:38 p.m.

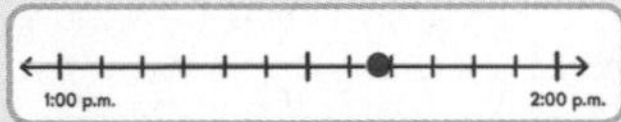

page 95
The land of Nod is the poet's dreams. Stanza one states that the poet goes there at night, stanza two states that the poet goes "up the mountainsides of dreams," and stanza three states that the poet is there until morning.
a real place in another country
strange things to eat and see, and also frightening sights and curious music
The poet says that he can't find a way back to Nod, and that he often can't remember the details.

page 97
Comanche and Apache
Massachuset
No; Seminole
Cherokee

page 100
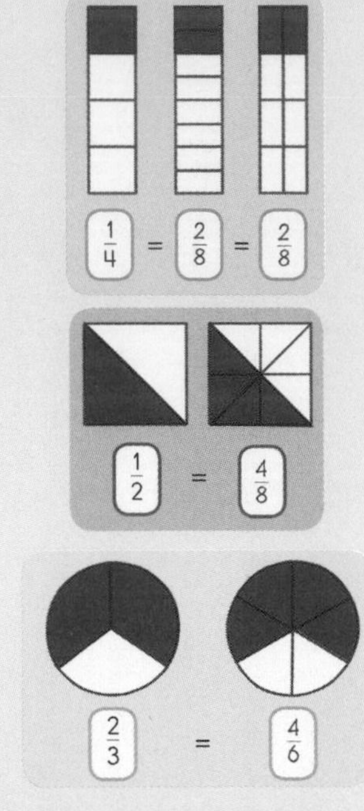

BONUS: Answers will vary.

page 101
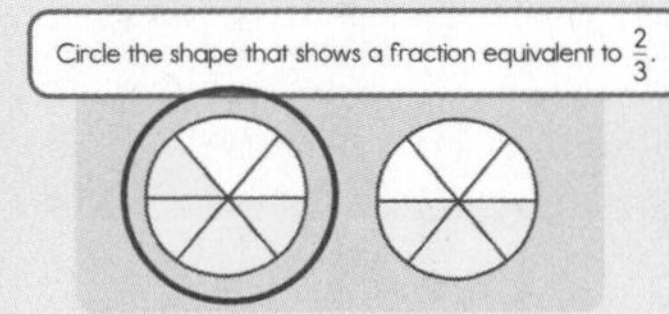

Circle the shape that shows a fraction equivalent to $\frac{2}{3}$.

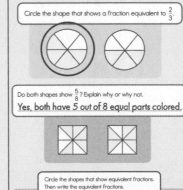

Do both shapes show $\frac{5}{8}$? Explain why or why not.
Yes, both have 5 out of 8 equal parts colored.

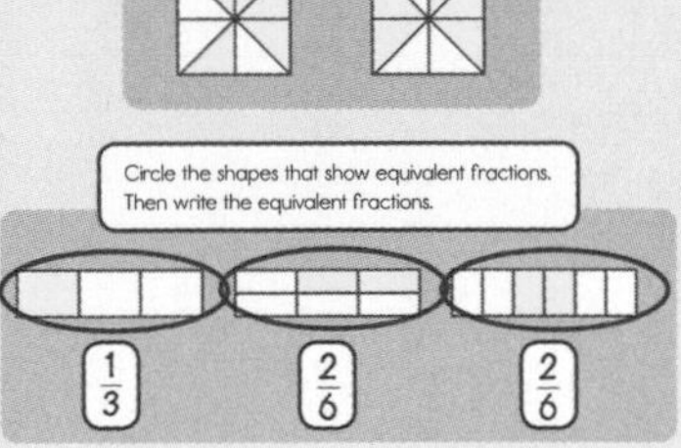

Circle the shapes that show equivalent fractions. Then write the equivalent fractions.
$\frac{1}{3}$
$\frac{2}{6}$
$\frac{2}{6}$

page 102
terrified; answers will vary.
overjoyed; answers will vary.
furious; answers will vary.
upset; answers will vary.
miserable; answers will vary.
thrilled; answers will vary.
exhausted; answers will vary.
rare; answers will vary.

page 103
suspected
stories
wondered
descend
village
heard
BONUS: dark

page 104
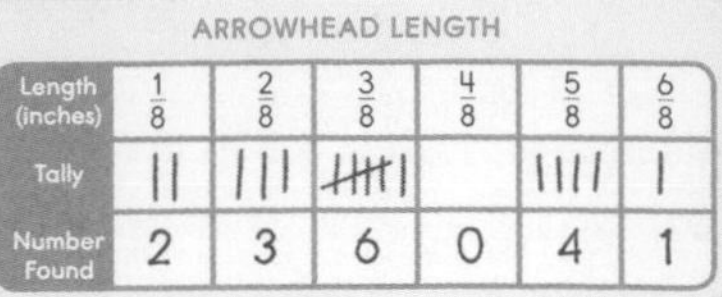

ARROWHEAD LENGTH

Length (inches)	$\frac{1}{8}$	$\frac{2}{8}$	$\frac{3}{8}$	$\frac{4}{8}$	$\frac{5}{8}$	$\frac{6}{8}$
Tally	||	|||	卌|		||||	|
Number Found	2	3	6	0	4	1

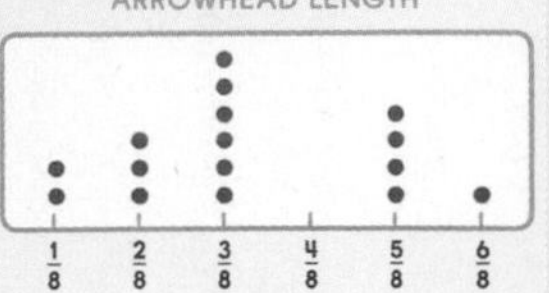

$\frac{3}{8}$
$\frac{4}{8}$
16

LEVEL 6

page 107
legs
tentacles
wings
fur
rain
because it can adapt its behavior to make nests in either place
A giant squid could not survive on land because its respiratory system cannot extract oxygen from the air (only from the water), and its tentacles would not be very good for movement on land.
Answers will vary.
Answers will vary.

page 108
1, 3, 5, 7, 9, 11, 13
Any of the following answers: They are all odd numbers; each number is 2 more than the one before.
26, 28, 30, 32, 34, 36
Any of the following answers: They are all even numbers; each number is 2 more than the one before.
18, 27, 36, 45, 54, 63
Any of the following answers: They are the times table for 9; the digits in each number add up to 9; each number is 9 more than the one before.

pages 110–111
Members of Congress are elected in two different ways: the members of the Senate get their jobs by being elected by the states, while the members of the House of Representatives are elected by their districts.

The legislative branch makes our country's laws, while the judicial branch interprets the laws and determines if they are constitutional.

	House of Representatives	Senate	Supreme Court	President
Branch of government	legislative	legislative	judicial	executive
Role	makes laws	makes laws	interprets laws	enforces laws
Term of Service	2 years	6 years	lifetime	4 or 8 years

BONUS: the Senate and the House of Representatives

page 113

taking night excursions under disguise

No. He keeps his plans secret from his vizier.

the sultan's baker

so she can eat her fill of bread

the sultan's cook

so she can eat her fill of excellent food

hair that is half-silver and half-gold, tears like pearls, lips like a rosebud

Answers will vary.

pages 114–115

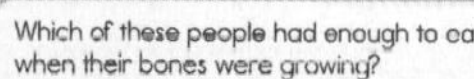

Which of these people had enough to eat when their bones were growing?

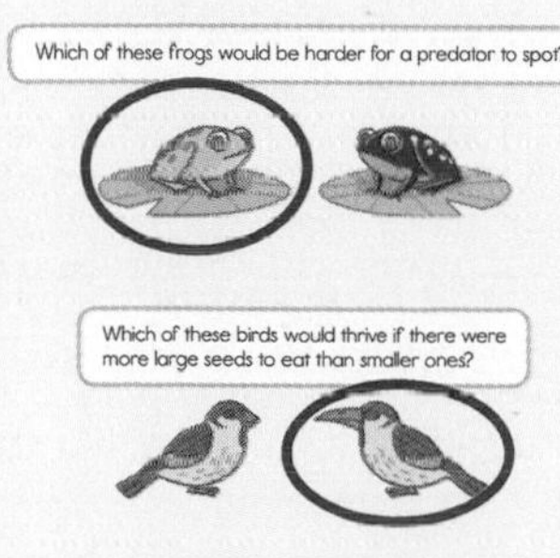

Which of these frogs would be harder for a predator to spot?
Which of these birds would thrive if there were more large seeds to eat than smaller ones?

Which of these squirrels would survive best if they both had to migrate to a city where the buildings are mostly gray?

BONUS: Answers will vary. Sample: the need for defense, digging, or chewing

page 116

$7 \times 2 = 14$; 14

$4 \times 3 = 12$; 12

$2 \times 10 = 20$; 20

page 117

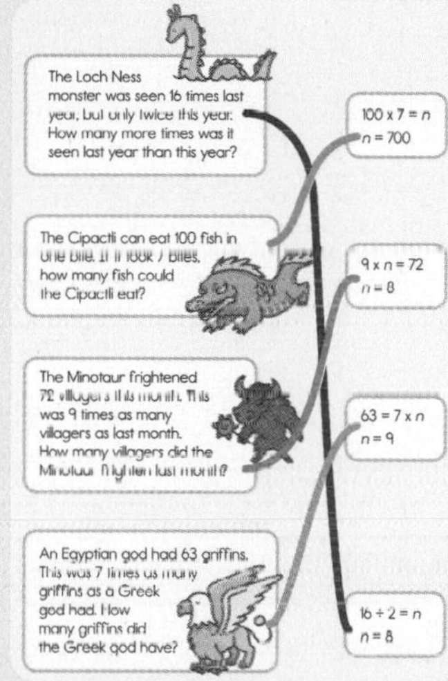

The Loch Ness monster was seen 16 times last year, but only twice this year. How many more times was it seen last year than this year?
The Cipactli can eat 100 fish in one bite. If it took 7 bites, how many fish could the Cipactli eat?
The Minotaur frightened 72 villagers this month. This was 9 times as many villagers as last month. How many villagers did the Minotaur frighten last month?
An Egyptian god had 63 griffins. This was 7 times as many griffins as a Greek god had. How many griffins did the Greek god have?
100 x 7 = n
n = 700
9 x n = 72
n = 8
63 = 7 x n
n = 9
16 ÷ 2 = n
n = 8

page 118

Circle the smallest set of figures that repeat.

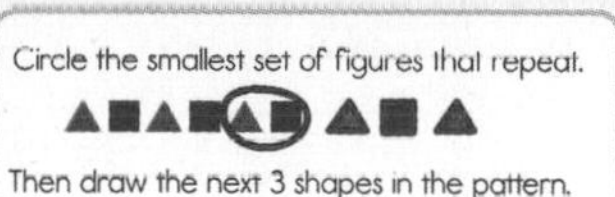

Then draw the next 3 shapes in the pattern.

Circle the smallest set of figures that repeat.

Then draw the next 4 shapes in the pattern.

Circle the smallest set of figures that repeat.

Then draw the next 5 shapes in the pattern.

BONUS: Answers will vary.

page 119

his mother, Thetis, dipped him in the magical River Styx.

the water wasn't able to coat his heel and it wasn't protected.

the arrow killed him.

page 121

The city is noisier.

Any three of the following details: Everyone was in bed; no wagons were in the streets; no people shouted; the policemen slept; there were no thieves.

One time, Finally, Therefore, So at the proper time, During his wanderings, So, Then

"Fly away, my beauties, and be happy again!"

He wants the birds to be free and happy.

Answers will vary.

pages 124–125

$3 \times 12 = 36$; $36 - 16 = 20$; 20

$4 \times 6 = 24$; $9 \times 6 = 54$; $24 + 54 = 78$; 78

$4 \times 7 = 28$; $2 \times 8 = 16$; $28 + 16 = 44$; $44 \div 4 = 11$; 11

BONUS: Answers will vary. Sample: Hermes had 10 pairs of red winged shoes and 30 pairs of green winged shoes. How many single shoes did he have in all? $2 \times 10 + 2 \times 30 = 20 + 60 = 80$ single shoes

$156 - 132 = 24$; $24 \div 2 = 12$; 12

$250 - 200 = 50$; $50 \div 10 = 5$; 5

$2 \times 25 = 50$; $50 + 25 = 75$; 75

page 126

Coal power comes from the energy released when coal is burned. The raw coal is mined from deposits buried in the earth.

Solar power captures the energy of the sun, through panels that absorb sunshine and turn it into energy that can be used as electrical power in homes and businesses.

Wind power harnesses the power of the strong breezes that move across the face of the planet. These gusts turn giant turbines, which in turn create electricity.

Natural gas power comes from deposits of flammable gas trapped deep underground. To release the energy, the gas is burned, and its heat is used to generate electricity.

Hydro power comes from the force of water rushing over dams that are built to contain the flow of a river. The power of the water turns giant turbines, which in turn create electricity.

Summer Brain Quest Extras

Stay smart all sumer long with these Summer Brain Quest Extras! In this section you'll find:

Summer Brain Quest Reading List

A book can take you anywhere—and summer is a great time to go on a reading adventure! Use the Summer Brain Quest Reading List to help you start the next chapter of your quest!

Summer Brain Quest Mini Deck

Cut out the cards and make your own Summer Brain Quest Mini Deck. Play by yourself or with a friend.

Summer Brain Quest Reading List

We recommend reading at least 15 to 30 minutes each day. Read to yourself or aloud. You can also read aloud with a friend or family member and discuss the book. Here are some questions to get you started:

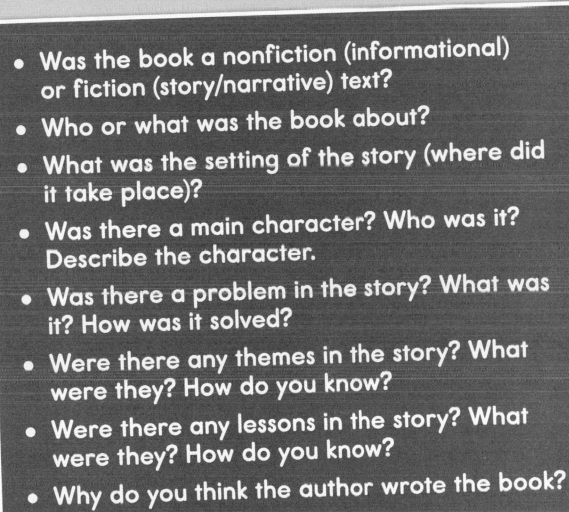

- Was the book a nonfiction (informational) or fiction (story/narrative) text?
- Who or what was the book about?
- What was the setting of the story (where did it take place)?
- Was there a main character? Who was it? Describe the character.
- Was there a problem in the story? What was it? How was it solved?
- Were there any themes in the story? What were they? How do you know?
- Were there any lessons in the story? What were they? How do you know?
- Why do you think the author wrote the book?

Jump-start your reading adventure by visiting your local library or bookstore and checking out the following books. Track which ones you've read, and write your own review! Would you recommend this book to a friend? If so, which friend would you recommend this book to, and why?

Fiction

The BFG, written by Roald Dahl, illustrated by Quentin Blake

When Sophie is kidnapped by a giant, she's scared . . . until she realizes her kidnapper is a Big Friendly Giant—a BFG! Together they hatch a plan to save children from the bigger, meaner giants.

DATE STARTED: ______________________ **DATE FINISHED:** ______________________

MY REVIEW: ____

____

Bink and Gollie, written by Kate DiCamillo and Alison McGhee, illustrated by Tony Fucile

Meet Bink and Gollie, two best friends who are opposites of each other. Join them on their adventures as they skate around and get into shenanigans.

DATE STARTED: ______________________ **DATE FINISHED:** ______________________

MY REVIEW: ____

____

Cleopatra VII: Daughter of the Nile (The Royal Diaries #1), by Kristiana Gregory

Travel back in time with this fearless pharaoh and explore ancient Egypt and Rome. This 12-year-old's diary documents her meeting people like Caesar, Marc Antony, and Cicero.

DATE STARTED: ______________________ **DATE FINISHED:** ______________________

MY REVIEW: ____

____

D'Aulaires' Book of Greek Myths, by Ingri and Edgar d'Aulaire

Ever wonder what gods and goddesses do all day? Follow this supernatural family as they get into—and cause—ungodly trouble.

DATE STARTED: ____________________ **DATE FINISHED:** ____________________

MY REVIEW: ____

____

Hamster and Cheese (Guinea Pig, Pet Shop Private Eye #1), written by Colleen AF Venable, illustrated by Stephanie Yue

Someone is stealing sandwiches, and Sasspants, the pet store's very own guinea pig private eye, is going to get to the bottom of it. With the help of her sidekick, Hamisher the Hamster, Sasspants sorts through all the suspects—a pet shop full of outrageous animals.

DATE STARTED: ____________________ **DATE FINISHED:** ____________________

MY REVIEW: ____

____

Lulu and the Brontosaurus, written by Judith Viorst, illustrated by Lane Smith

Lulu is used to getting what she wants, so when her parents decide to not give her a brontosaurus for her birthday, she heads out to find her own. But what will she do when the dinosaur decides he wants *her* to be *his* pet? Choose between three endings to decide Lulu's fate.

DATE STARTED: ____________________ **DATE FINISHED:** ____________________

MY REVIEW: ____

____

My Diary from the Edge of the World, by Jodi Lynn Anderson

Read the diary of Gracie Lockwood, a normal girl who lives in a not-so-normal world—one filled with malls and fast food, but also dragons, Sasquatches, and more! When an ominous cloud appears over her family's home, they set out to cross over into our world by matching science with magic.

DATE STARTED: ______________________ **DATE FINISHED:** ______________________

MY REVIEW: ____

____

Pink and Say by Patricia Polacco

Pink and Say are two boys fighting for the Union army in confederate territory. Together they face danger, make tough decisions, and ultimately confront the heartbreak of war.

DATE STARTED: ______________________ **DATE FINISHED:** ______________________

MY REVIEW: ____

____

The Quest Begins (Seekers #1), by Erin Hunter

Three different bears leave home on a journey led by the North Star. They have to band together if they want to make it through their dangerous voyage.

DATE STARTED: ______________________ **DATE FINISHED:** ______________________

MY REVIEW: ____

____

Roller Girl, by Victoria Jamieson

Astrid has fallen in love with roller derby, but Nicole, the friend she does *everything* with, has not. Now these best friends are going to different camps and making other friends. Can their friendship last?

DATE STARTED: ______________________ **DATE FINISHED:** ______________________

MY REVIEW: ____

____

Nonfiction

The Boy Who Harnessed the Wind, by William Kamkwamba and Bryan Mealer

When famine strikes the country of Malawi, William is forced to drop out of school to help his family survive. Armed with his imagination and lots of library books, he invents a windmill that helps his family thrive.

DATE STARTED: ______________________ **DATE FINISHED:** ______________________

MY REVIEW: ____

____

The Book Itch: Freedom, Truth, and Harlem's Greatest Bookstore, written by Vaunda Micheaux Nelson, illustrated by R. Gregory Christie

When Lewis's father got a book itch, he scratched it by starting a bookstore in Harlem called the National Memorial African Bookstore. It drew visitors from Muhammad Ali to Malcolm X.

DATE STARTED: ______________________ **DATE FINISHED:** ______________________

MY REVIEW: ____

____

Colossal Paper Machines: Make 10 Giant Models That Move!, by Phil Conigliaro and Theo Baker

While you learn all about the history and mechanics behind each of these machines, you get to build paper models of them that actually move!

DATE STARTED: ______________________ **DATE FINISHED:** ______________________

MY REVIEW: ____

____

The Day-Glo Brothers, written by Chris Barton, illustrated by Tony Persiani

Imagine inventing a new color. Two brothers did just that! Read about their process and how their discovery changed the world.

DATE STARTED: ____________________ **DATE FINISHED:** ____________________

MY REVIEW: ____________________

____

Girls Think of Everything: Stories of Ingenious Inventions by Women, written by Catherine Thimmesh, illustrated by Melissa Sweet

Girls have created some amazing things, from white-out correction fluid and windshield wipers to so much more! Read about the people behind the inventions and get a start on making your own ideas a reality.

DATE STARTED: ____________________ **DATE FINISHED:** ____________________

MY REVIEW: ____________________

____

How Do You Burp in Space?, written by Susan E. Goodman, illustrated by Michael Slack

Space tourism is right around the corner, and this book will help you prepare for your trip. What should you pack? Where will you sleep? What activities can you do? Study up for your own space odyssey.

DATE STARTED: ____________________ **DATE FINISHED:** ____________________

MY REVIEW: ____________________

____

How to Tell a Story: 1 Book + 20 Story Blocks = A Million Adventures, written by Daniel Nayeri, illustrated by Brian Won

In this book and blocks set, each block represents an element of storytelling, from characters to conflict. Read the book about how to tell a story, then roll the blocks to start a never-ending adventure!

DATE STARTED: ____________________ DATE FINISHED: ____________________

MY REVIEW: ____

____

I Survived True Stories: Five Epic Disasters, by Lauren Tarshis

These kids survived some of the craziest, scariest situations imaginable. In the midst of a blizzard, a sinking ship—even a flood of molasses—these kids escaped with their lives! How did they do it?

DATE STARTED: ____________________ DATE FINISHED: ____________________

MY REVIEW: ____

____

The Kid from Diamond Street, written by Audrey Vernick, illustrated by Steven Salerno

Edith Houghton is only 10 years old when she starts playing for a professional women's baseball team. Will she be able to compete against full-grown male baseball players?

DATE STARTED: ____________________ DATE FINISHED: ____________________

MY REVIEW: ____

____

We Are the Ship: The Story of Negro League Baseball,
by Kadir Nelson

Before the civil rights movement, even sports teams were segregated. Follow these athletes as they overcome hatred, follow their dreams, and change the world!

DATE STARTED: ______________ DATE FINISHED: ______________

MY REVIEW: ______________

____

And don't stop here! There's a whole world to discover. All you need is a book!

Summer Brain Quest Mini Deck

QUESTIONS

A sailor sees 7 schools of fish. There are 8 fish in each group. How many fish did he see in all?

Should the name of a city be capitalized or not?

What is the best solution for erosion that is due to high winds: sandbags, windbreaks, or lightning rods?

Is a person who was there when an event happened a primary or a secondary source?

QUESTIONS

There are 28 chariot wheels. If each chariot has 4 wheels, how many chariots are there?

Is it *literally* true that you can die of boredom?

What sense does a praying mantis use through its antennae?

Who led the movement for India's independence from Britain?

QUESTIONS

Medusa had 98 snakes on her head. How many snakes is that to the nearest ten? How many is it to the nearest hundred?

Which of these would you not use to support an opinion: detail, facts, rhyme, reason?

If a baseball hits a basketball, will some of the baseball's energy make the basketball move?

True or false: It doesn't matter what order events go in on a timeline, as long as they're all there.

QUESTIONS

There are 11 unicorns in a row. How many horns are there?

What superlative finishes this set: good, better, ______ ?

True or false: A person could survive in any environment.

Is money a natural resource, a human resource, or a capital resource?

ANSWERS

 7 chariots

 no

 touch

 Mahatma Gandhi

ANSWERS

 56 fish

 capitalized

 windbreaks

 a primary source

ANSWERS

 11 horns

 best

 false

 a capital resource

ANSWERS

 100; 100

 rhyme

 yes

 false

QUESTIONS

What multiplication property says that 6 x 8 = 8 x 6?

Is the "in" in "invisible" a prefix or a suffix?

If you found a fish fossil in the desert, could there have once been water there?

Who won the Nobel Prize for pioneering work on radioactivity?

QUESTIONS

A rectangular lake is 3 miles wide and 5 miles long. What is the area of the lake?

True or false: A sentence doesn't need a verb, just a subject.

Does a lightbulb use electric or magnetic energy?

A forest is what kind of resource?

QUESTIONS

Hermes traveled 627 miles by sea and 212 miles on land. How many miles did he travel in total?

Which of these is a preposition: "in" or "outdoors"?

What part of an elephant uses the same sense as the human nose?

What document is the foundation of all laws in the United States?

QUESTIONS

A longhouse is 180 feet long and 20 feet wide. What is the perimeter of the longhouse?

What is the common root word in "telegraph" and "phonograph"?

True or false: Using natural fuels is good for the environment because they're natural.

The judicial branch of government is made up of what?

ANSWERS

 15 square miles

 false

 electric energy

 a natural resource

ANSWERS

 commutative property

 a prefix

 yes

 Marie Curie

ANSWERS

 400 feet

 graph

 false

 judges and the courts

ANSWERS

 839 miles

 in

 the trunk

 The Constitution

QUESTIONS

If a pyramid has a square base, how many triangular faces does it have?

Does a compound sentence have one subject or two?

Is tropical a season or a climate?

What is the name of the king who turned Timbuktu into a center of learning?

QUESTIONS

If you saw 57 ancient ruins and 38 ancient castles, how many more ruins did you see than castles?

What is the first step in research, finding an answer or asking a question?

What do we call power produced by the sun?

What wooden animal did the Greeks leave outside of Troy?

QUESTIONS

Chronos began harvesting wheat at 4:15 p.m. and worked for 42 minutes, at what time did he finish?

Is a stanza part of a poem or a story?

Is coal a renewable or a nonrenewable energy source?

True or false: The Iroquois Nation elected representatives to lead their democracy.

QUESTIONS

Which traveler has more—a traveler with a 3-liter jug that is $\frac{3}{8}$ full or a traveler that has a 3-liter jug that is $\frac{5}{8}$ full?

How do you fix a run-on sentence?

When something is going fast, does it have more energy than something that is going slow?

What tells you directions on a map?

ANSWERS

19

asking a question

solar power

a horse

ANSWERS

4

two

a climate

Mansa Musa

ANSWERS

The traveler with the jug that is $\frac{5}{8}$ full; $\frac{5}{8} > \frac{3}{8}$

You separate it into different sentences.

yes

the compass rose

ANSWERS

4:57 p.m.

a poem

a nonrenewable source

true

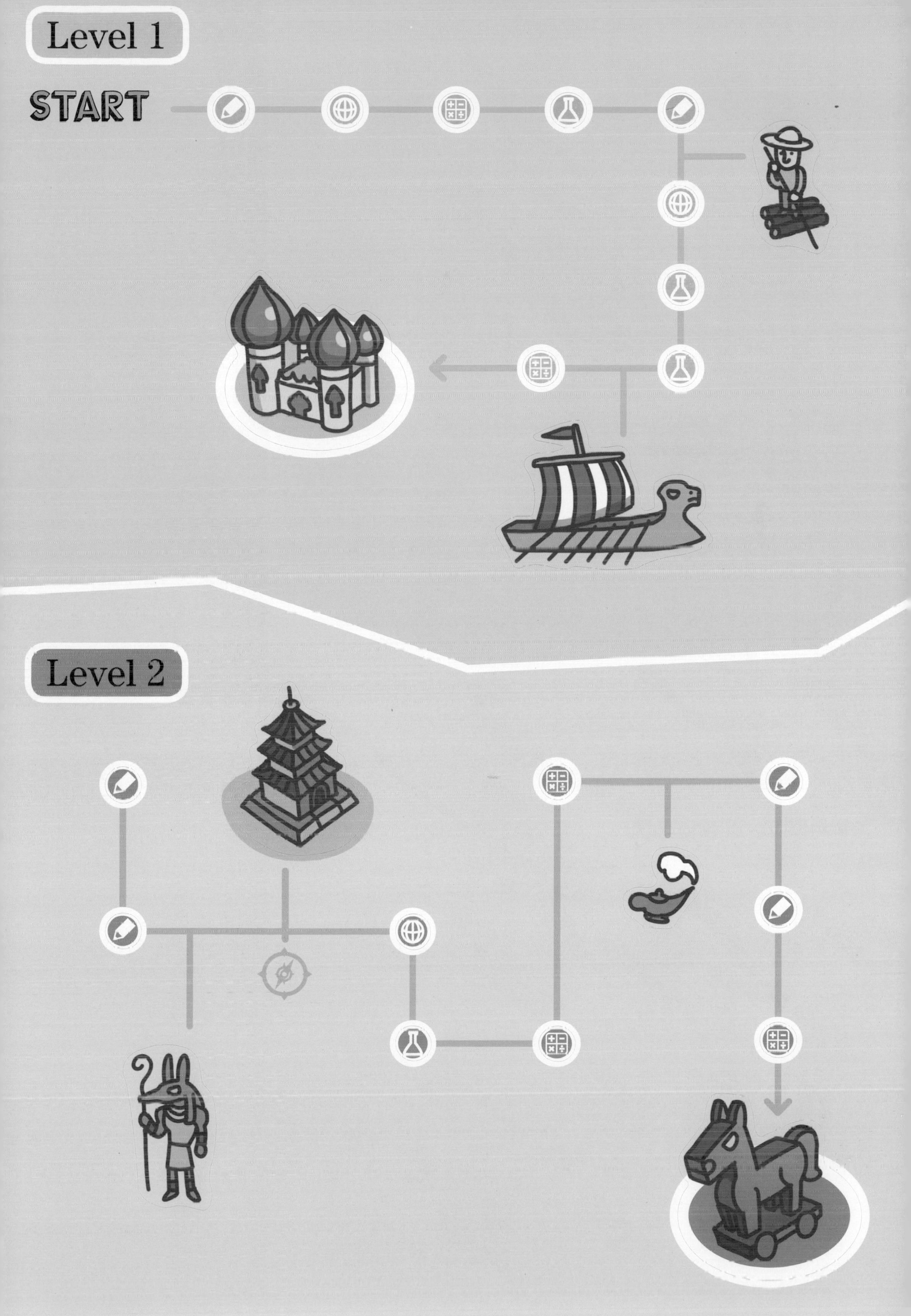

Level 1

START

Level 2

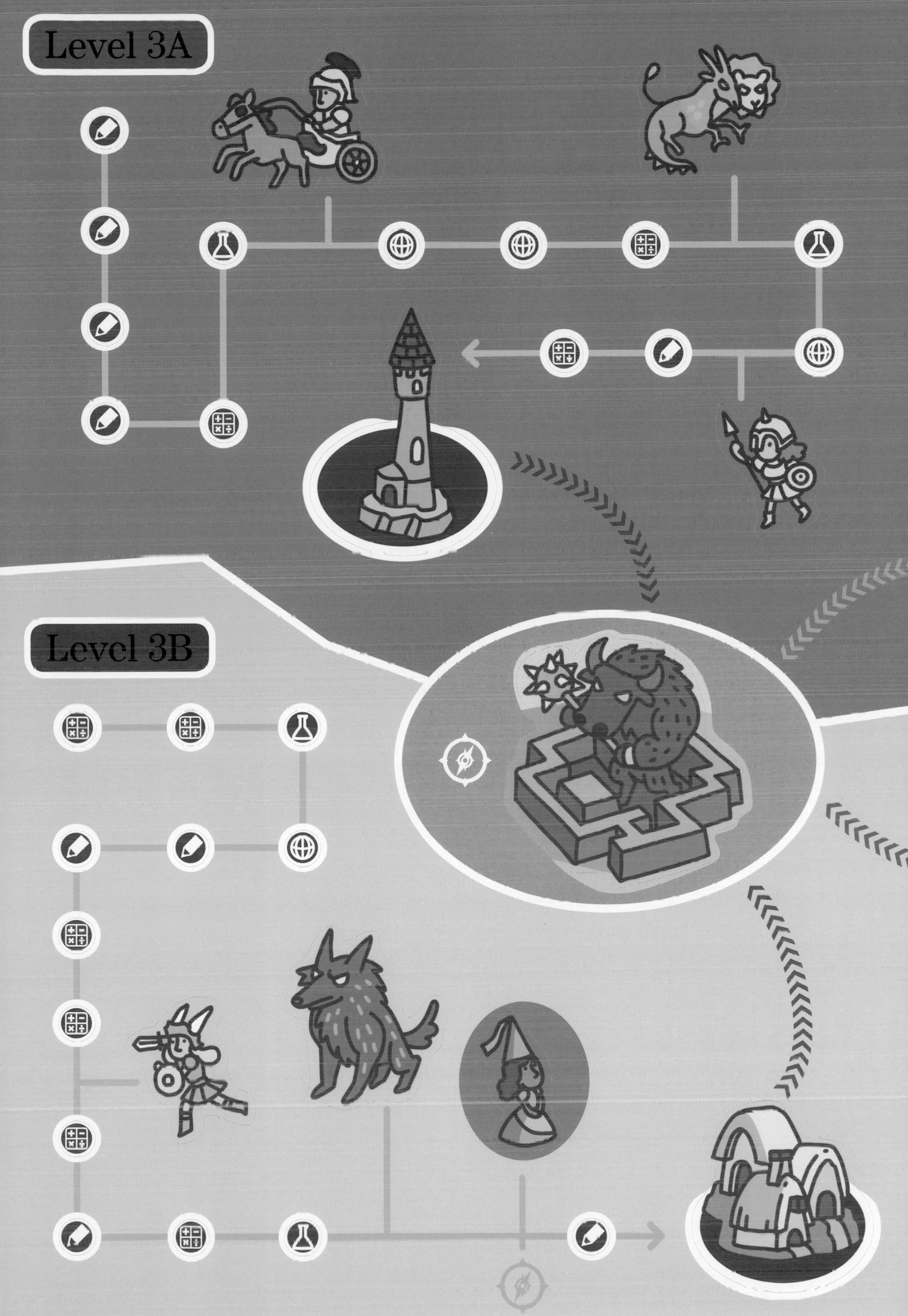
Level 3A
Level 3B

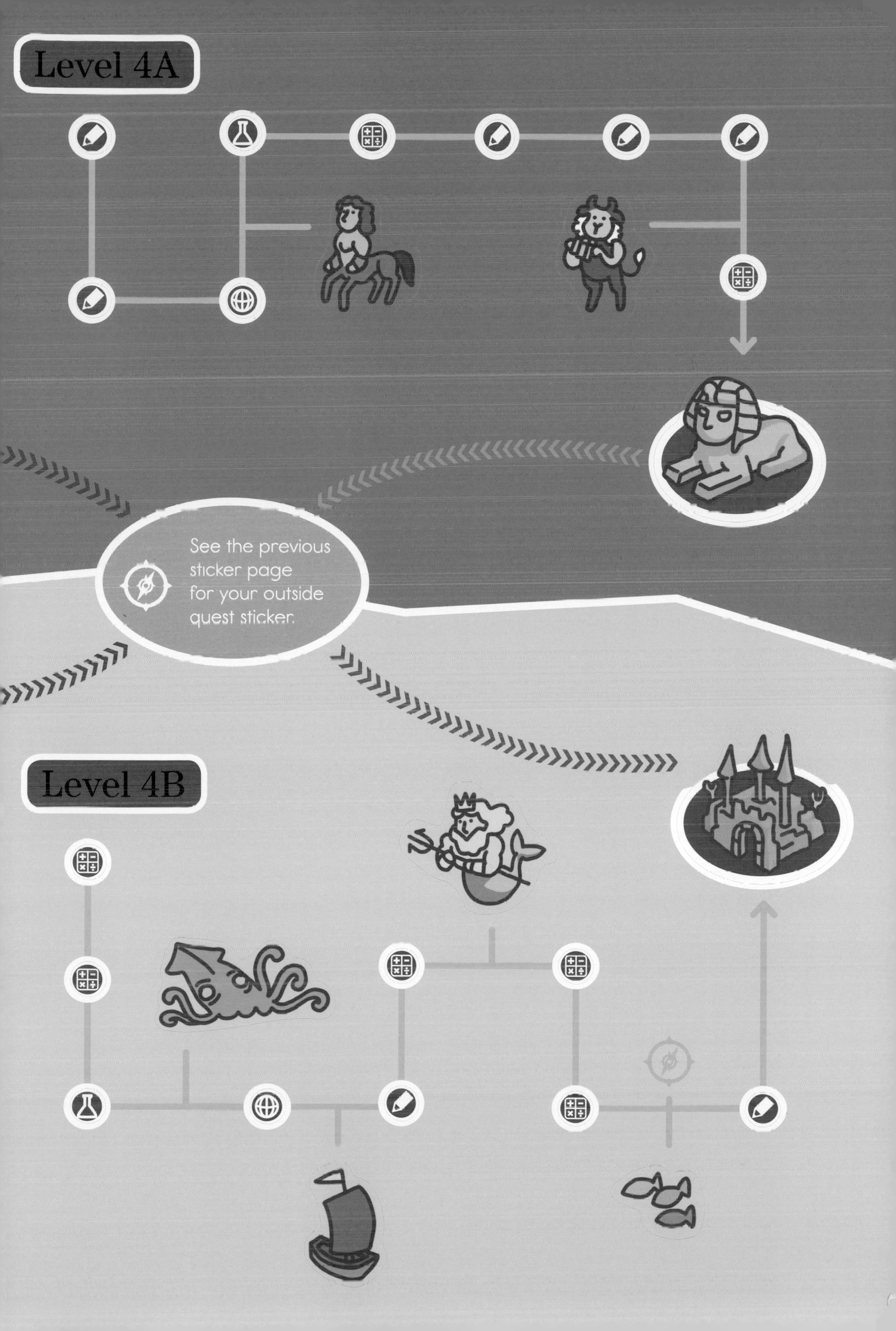

Level 4A

See the previous sticker page for your outside quest sticker.

Level 4B

Level 5A
Level 5B

Level 6

QUEST
complete!
Welcome to
4th grade!

Did you sticker **every** route possible and finish **all** the Outside Quests? What an achievement!

You've earned the **100% STICKER!**